"Deel Leit meene, ass die Zeit schunt verbei iss, wu die Pennsylvaanisch-Deitsche alliwwer in Natt America Bicher in die Mudderschprooch gschriwwe un gedruckt henn—un ass die deitsch Schprooch ball zu nix geht.

"Isaac Horst weist mit seim Bichli, ass sell net recht iss— un ass mer aa im 21. Yaahrhunnert noch ebbes Guudes in deitsch schreiwe un drucke kann. Sei Bichli *Bei sich selwer un ungwehnlich* iss verleicht 's beschte, was in die letschte Yaahre in Pennsylvaanisch-Deitsch gschriwwe iss warre. Wann ebber gleiche deet, en wennich ebbes lanne, vun wie die Fuhremennischte in Ontario lewe, sett er sell Bichli lese. Was Isaac Horst gschriwwe hot, iss ebbes waricklich Abaddiches."

—*Dr. Michael Werner, Ober-Olm, Deutschland*
  Schriftleiter, Hiwwe wie Driwwe
  (Die Pennsylvaanisch Deitsch Zeiding)

"Some people suppose that the time is already past when Pennsylvania Germans all over North America write and print books in the mother tongue, and that the German language is almost going to nothing.

"Through his book, Isaac Horst shows that this is not true—and that in the twenty-first century something good can still be written and printed in German. His book *Separate and Peculiar* is possibly the best that has been written in Pennsylvania German in recent years. Whoever wants to learn something of how the team Mennonites in Ontario live should read this book. What Isaac Horst wrote is truly something special."

—*Dr. Michael Werner, Ober-Olm, Germany;*
  Editor, Hiwwe wie Driwwe
  (The Pennsylvania German Magazine)

Herald Press Books
by Isaac R. Horst

A Separate People: An Insider's View
of Old Order Mennonite Customs and Traditions

Separate and Peculiar:
Old Order Mennonite Life in Ontario

Separate and Peculiar

Bei sich selwer un ungwehnlich

Bei sich selwer un ungwehnlich

Alt Mennischde Weg vun Lewe in Ontario

Zwett Auflage

Isaac R. Horst

Herald
Press

Waterloo, Ontario
Scottdale, Pennsylvania

Separate and Peculiar

Old Order Mennonite Life in Ontario

Second Edition

Isaac R. Horst

Herald
Press

Waterloo, Ontario
Scottdale, Pennsylvania

Canadian Cataloguing-in-Publication Data
Horst, Isaac R., 1918-
    Separate and peculiar : Old Order Mennonite life in Ontario = Bei sich
selwer un ungwehnlich : alt Mennischde Weg vun Lewe in Ontario
2nd ed. = 2. Aufl.
Text in English and Pennsylvania German.
Includes bibliographical references.
ISBN 0-8361-9146-3
1. Mennonites—Ontario—Woolwich. I. Title. II. Title: Bei sich selwer un
ungwehnlich.
FC3100.M45H64 2001   305.6'87071344   C00-933002-X
F1059.7.M45H64 2001

English Scripture is from the King James Version, with adaptations toward current
usage. German Scripture is from *Die Bibel*, translated by Martin Luther.

The cover art *Playing in the Snow* is from an original painting by Peter Etril Snyder,
a Canadian artist who has painted Mennonite country life as well as scenes in
Canada and Europe for the past thirty years. More of his work can be seen on the
Internet: www.snyder-gallery.com.

First edition only in English, copyright © 1979 by Isaac R. Horst, with ISBN
0-969090978-1-6. Reprinted Nov. 1983. This bilingual and expanded second edition
(2001) is in Pennsylvania German and English.

Copyright clearance information appears on page 9.

SEPARATE AND PECULIAR
BEI SICH SELWER UN UNGWEHNLICH
Second edition, bilingual, copyright © 2001 by Herald Press, Waterloo,
    Ont. N2L 6H7. Published simultaneously in USA by Herald Press,
    Scottdale, Pa. 15683. All rights reserved
Canadiana Entry Number: C00-933002-X
Library of Congress Catalog Card Number: 00-110251
International Standard Book Number: 0-8361-9146-3
Printed in the United States of America
Cover art by Peter Etril Snyder/Inside illustrations by Edwin B. Wallace
Book cover and design by Gwen M. Stamm

10 09 08 07 06 05 04 03 02 01 10 9 8 7 6 5 4 3 2 1

To order or request information, please call 1-800-759-4447 (individuals);
1-800-245-7894 (trade). Website: www.mph.org

Come out from among them, and be separate,
says the Lord.

Gehet aus von ihnen und sondert euch ab,
spricht der Herr.

—2 Corinthians 6:17

You are a chosen generation
a royal priesthood,
a holy nation,
a peculiar people.

Ihr seid das auserwählte Geschlecht,
das königliche Priestertum,
das heilige Volk,
das Volk des Eigentums.

—1 Peter 2:9

Inhalt

Contents

Vorwatt

DES BUCH gebt em Leser en guder Blick in es Lewe vun der Altmennischde in Ontario. Die mennischde Leit vun ausser der Gmee verschtehn ihre Lewe un Addninge gar net. Sie sehne die Altmennischde als en Aart vun abgfallene Amische, un doch hen die Alde Amische net viel Eifluss gebraucht iwwer die Altmennischde. Yeder Altmennischde Gmee hot sei eegne Herkummes, un deswege sei eegne Eigenschafder.

Ihm sei erschde Gedanke waere das des Buch waer gschriwwe fer die wo so Leit net bekannt sin. Doch wann mir Acht hot uff die unnerschiedliche Gebrauche bei verschiedene Gegende, seht mir das sie wohl net gleich sin. Deel schtehn scharf raus; annere sin Gleenichkeide.

Een exembel waer der Breddichschtul wo gebraucht waet in der Ontario Versammlingheiser. Die Altmennischde in Pennsilfaani hen en Breddichdisch fer die Diener, un en Singdisch fer die Vorsinger. Noch en Unnerschied is das in Ontario lest der Eldeschder der Text *erscht* ab, un dann kummt die Vorreed; in Pennsilfaani kummt die Vorreed erscht.

In em Buchschtawwiere hot es aa unnerschiedliche Wege fer sich ausschpreche. Eens kann gesehne sei in em Naame vun dem Buch: *Bei sich selwer*. In Pennsilfaani waet es ausgschproche als *Bei sich selwert*. Doch kann yeder Gegend sei eegne Addning hawwe, was sie recht odder letz heese.

Bei dem lese hab ich viel Wadde glaennt wo net gebraucht waerre in Lengeschder Kaundi. Ich muss saage mir waare gross eignumme mit wie fellich die Sache beschriwwe sin in dem Buch. Es hot net viel Bicher wo der Schreiwer so gut weest vun was er schwetzt odder schreibt. Der Isaac Horst is net

Foreword

THIS BOOK gives readers a good view into the lives of the Old Order Mennonites (OOMs) of Ontario. Most of the "outsider" people do not really understand Old Order Mennonite lives and customs. They often perceive OOMs as being a type of renegade Amish, although the Old Order Amish have influenced the Old Order Mennonites very little. Yet each OOM locality has its specific background and thus has its own characteristics.

One's first impression is that this book was especially designed for nonplain people or outsiders. But if one actually compares the variety of practices in the various settlements, one notices differences. Some are obvious points, and others are small and subtle customs that have arisen.

The author touches on one striking example: a pulpit is used by the OOMs in Canada; in Pennsylvania, however, an OOM meetinghouse has a preacher's table and a song leader's table. Another sharp contrast is how the deacon reads the Scripture text *before* the introductory sermon in Ontario; with us in Pennsylvania, the text is read *afterward*.

Minute differences have also crept into our speech. One example can be seen on the title page of this book: *Bei sich selwer*, meaning "Separated." In Pennsylvania, one would think a letter *t* is missing, and that it should read *Bei sich selwert*. But certainly each community has the right to set its own criteria for proper pronunciation. By reading this book, I have learned many words that are not common in Lancaster County, Pennsylvania.

I was greatly impressed with the fine details found through-

yuscht en guder Friend: er is aa en erfahrener Schtudent vun dem Altmennischde Lewe, un aa im alt Deitsch Schreiwes iwwersetze.

Mit seim achtzich Yaahr Erfahring in dem, bin ich ganz sicher das des Buch net yuscht en Schtori is wo leicht owwerdriwwe geht. Ich bin sicher das des es menscht Wertwoll Schreiwes is das mir griege kann, in Pennsilfaani Deitsch un Englisch, alles in ee Buch.

Die Vizepresidentin vun Deitschland hot en Rees gnumme darich unser Gegend in 1983, un sie war ganz eignumme in dem, das es noch 300 Yaahr, alsnoch Deitsche Leit hot in Amerika.

Es is zum lowe das die Altmennischde in der Schteets un in Kanadaa alsnoch Bekanntschaft hen minanne noch 200 Yaahr, wie des Buch beweisst. Des is ganz grischtlich, un wunderbar schee.

Lees weider mit vergniege.

—*Amos B. Hoover, den 20ten Yenner im Jahr Christi 2001*
Von der Moddigrick
Denver, Pennsilfaani

out the book. There are not many books on the market where the author knows from the inside so well what he is talking or writing about. Isaac Horst is my good friend; he also is an accomplished scholar, precisely in the subject area of Old Order Mennonites. This is true because he is part of the OOMs in real life and because he has been translating Mennonite documents of yore. With his eighty years of experience, I am sure that this historical narrative is not superficial. Certainly this is the most important work to ever be available simultaneously in both Pennsylvania German and English.

Germany's vice-president made a trip into our area in 1983 and was visibly moved to find an alive German culture after three hundred years in America. She exclaimed that she finds this enchanting.

Likewise, I observe that for two hundred years the Old Order Mennonites of North America are still in contact with each other across the international border, between Lancaster in the United States, and Ontario in Canada, as this book confirms. This is nothing short of a miracle. It is our Christian duty to keep this fellowship alive.

Read the book!

—*Amos B. Hoover, the 20th of January A.D. 2001*
Of the Muddy Creek
Denver, Pennsylvania

Vorreed

IN DEM das schunn viel sich vorgnumme hen fer die Sache wo mir draa glaawe antlich uffsetze, hab ich es fer gut aagsehne fer dir es aa antlich anneschreiwe, weil ich es gut verschtanne hab vum Aafang, so das du gwiss bischt vun der Sache" (Lukas 1:4).

Weil viel Leit eignumme sin alleweil in der unnerschiedliche Volksleit, will ich die Gebreiche, Glaawe, un Addninge vun unser Leit vorbringe, so das sie net en letze odder falsche Begriff griege davun.

In dem Buch browier ich sell duh wehe der Mennischde: besonders die Alt Mennischde wo in der Mitt vun suddwescht Ontario wuhne, in un um der Woolwich Bezirk, un noch weider fatt. Was glaawe sie? Wie lewe sie? Is es mieglich fer so eefach lewe, un als noch ziemlich froh sei? Uff der naegschde Bledder will ich die Froge antwadde.

Weil des Buch is wehe die Alt Mennischde, will ich noch dem sie yuscht Mennischde heese, fer es leichter mache fer der Schreiwer un der Leser. Sell soll ken Aaschtooss sei zu annere Mennischde in Ontario odder in Oscht Kanadaa wo Zammerkunfter hen, un hen sich selwer gschickt zu neuere Wege.

Viel vun der Gebreiche un Glaawe wo do beschriwwe sin, sin ehnlich zu die wo gebraucht waerre in annere Alt Mennischde un Amische Gegende, in Pennsilfaani, Ohio, un Indiana, un annere Schteets; yuscht Gebreiche verennere sich vun ee Gegend zu die anner.

Ich hab erwaehlt fer die Alt Mennischde Addninge vorlege darich es Lewe vun en Buh in der Gegend: der Menno Martin. *Menno* als der erscht Naame, un *Martin* als der letscht, sin

Preface

FORASMUCH as many have taken in hand to set forth in order a declaration of those things which are most surely believed among us, . . . it seemed good to me also, having had perfect understanding of all things from the very first, to write unto you, . . . that you might know the certainty of those things"(Luke 1:1-4).

Because the general public is showing so much interest in various ethnic groups, I want to place before the public a summary of the customs, beliefs, and culture of my people, to guard against observers forming false and misleading concepts.

In this book, I try to accomplish this task in relation to the Mennonites, specifically the Old Order Mennonites. These Old Orders live in the heart of southwestern Ontario, in and around the Municipality of Woolwich, and in outlying settlements. What do they believe? How do they function? Is it possible to live so austerely and still be relatively happy? These pages will answer these and other questions.

Since the Old Order Mennonites of Woolwich are the subjects of this book, I will henceforth refer to them only as Mennonites to make it easier for writer and reader. I intend no disrespect toward other Mennonites in Ontario and Eastern Canada, who have formed conferences and have adapted themselves more to modern culture.

Many of the beliefs and customs described here are similar to those of other Old Order Mennonites and Amish, in Pennsylvania, Ohio, Indiana, and various other states, though customs do vary somewhat from one community to another.

I have chosen to present the Old Order Mennonites through

bekannt bei unser Leit un kenne gut gebraucht waerre fer der Sinn rausbringe. Ich schreib wie wann es yetzt gschehe deet, so das der Leser es Mennischde Lewe graad mitmache kann, mit em Menno.

Weil des Buch is wehe der Ontario Mennischde wo aus Pennsilfaani gezoge sin, is es nadierlich fer die Iwwersetzing brauche wo bekannt is zu ihne. Noch zudem hab ich zehe Yaahr zugebrocht mit dem C. Richard Beam vun der Millerschtatt, Pennsilfaani, am Wadde ausleese.

Der Professor Beam hot der Buffington-Barba-Beam (BBB) Aart vun Buchschtawwiere verbessert, wo ich brauch beim Pennsilfaani Deitsch iwwersetze, mit noch gleeni Verbessringe noch em Ontario Ausschpreches.

—*Isaac R. Horst*
Der Isaak vun Bergwald
Mount Forest, Ontario, Kanada

describing some of the life cycle of a typical boy in our community, Menno Martin. *Menno* as a first name and *Martin* as a last name are popular among our people and will serve this storyteller well in representing the whole. I will also use the present tense to give readers a sense of experiencing Mennonite life along with Menno.

Since this book is about Ontario Mennonites who migrated from Pennsylvania, it is natural that in my translation, I use spelling that is familiar to them. In addition, for ten years I have been working on Pennsylvania German with C. Richard Beam, Millersville University, Pennsylvania. Professor Beam has refined the Buffington-Barba-Beam (BBB) spelling system I follow in my Pennsylvania German translation, with some adjustments for differing pronunciation in Ontario. I thank him for checking and polishing my translation in this book.

—*Isaac R. Horst*
Mt. Forest, Ontario, Canada

Die Kinneryaahre

W<small>ANN</small> der Menno Martin gebore is, is er net annerscht wie ennich anner Bobbi. Er hot graad so viel Aage, Ohre, Aerm, un Beh. Er schnauft un zwaerwelt un heilt. Sei Maem mehnt er is es menscht wunderbaar Ding fer eegene in der Welt. Sein Daed sehnt ihn als en zwaerweliche rode Bundel, zu gebrechlich fer haendle.

Sei Eldre hedde ihn aa James odder John odder Alvin odder Henry heese kenne. Sie hedde ihn aa Peter heese kenne, em Peter Martin nooch, wo der Vorvadder waar vun die Helft vun der Woolwich Mennischde. Odder David, em Peter sei Kossin, wo iwwer halwe so en grosse Noochkommeschaft hot wie der Peter. Der Peter hot siwwezeh Kinner ghat, un der David dreizeh. Ken Wunner das Martin Heiser so viel Deele hen!

Awwer sie hen ihn Menno Martin gheese. Der Menno waar em Menno Simons nooch-gheese, wo als en Paff waar, un wo die Mennischde schunn nooch-gheese waare, zerick in der 1500s, wo er ihrer Fiehrer waar. Sein letschder Naame, Martin, kennt schteh fer noch en Paff, der Martin Luther, wo die 95 These uff die Wittenberger Kariche Daer gnaggelt hot, in 1517.

Der Menno Simons hot erscht viel mit dem Luther zu duh ghat, awwer der Martin hot ghofft fer en Schtaat-Karich, wo gaar net dem Menno sein Sinn waar. Deswehe hen die Mennischde werklich schier so viel leide misse vun em Luther un sein Mithelfer, Ulrich Zwingli, wie vun der Gadollische.

Der Menno Martin is ken leibhafdicher Mensch. Er is yuscht en Figur vun der Mennischde. Er is yuscht *sich selwer un ungwehnlich*. Er is die ganze Mennischde zamme-gfasst. Er is so

The Childhood Years

WHEN Menno Martin is born, he is not different from any other baby. He has the same number of eyes, ears, arms, and legs. He breathes and wiggles and cries. His mother thinks he is the most precious possession in the world. His father sees him as a squirming red bundle, too fragile to handle.

His parents might have called him James or John or Alvin or Henry. They might even have called him Peter, after Peter Martin, the common ancestor of half of the Woolwich Mennonites. Or David, after Peter's cousin, with over half as many descendants as Peter. Peter had seventeen children and David thirteen. No wonder that Martin houses are built with many rooms!

But they called him Menno Martin. This Menno was the namesake of Menno Simons, the Anabaptist leader and former priest for whom the Mennonites were named way back in the 1500s. His last name, Martin, could stand for another former priest, Martin Luther, who nailed his ninety-five theses on the door of the Wittenberg church in 1517.

Menno Simons had much in common with Martin Luther, but Martin dreamed of a state church, an ambition Menno did not share. In fact, the followers of Menno Simons suffered almost as much persecution from Martin Luther and his accomplice, Ulrich Zwingli, as from the Catholics.

As an individual, Menno Martin does not exist. As a symbol, he is very real. He is *separate and peculiar*. He is a conglomerate of all Mennonites. He is the author's ancestor and descendant.

Menno is not very old when his peculiarities begin to show. He is not baptized as an infant. He has no godparents, no

zu saage, mein Vorvadder un mei Noochkummeschaft.
Der Menno is noch net arig alt bis es sich weisst das er ungwehnlich is. Er waet net gedaaft als en glee Kind. Er hot ken
Pedder, un ken Eiweihes. Weil sei Eldre Mennischde sin, waet
er gedaaft uff der Glaawe wann er die Elt hot fer antwattlich
zu sei. Des is eens vun der Glaawes-Regele wo er erbt vum
Menno Simons.

Es is wohl net das der Menno Simons der Glaawe aagfange
hot. Der Glaawe hot schunn aagfange an der Zeit vun der
Aposchdele. Die Kinnerdaaf hot nerscht aagfange am Cyprian
sei Zeit, zwee hunnert Yaahre schpeeder. Darich die naegschte
Yaahrhunnert hot es so zugnumme das yuscht noch en Finkli
vun dem alde Glaawe iwwerich waar. Im Yaahr 1160 hot der
Peter Waldo vun Lyons, Frankreich, es Daafe uff der Glaawe
widder uffgweckt. Fer iwwer en hunnert Yaahre hen die
Waldenser zugnumme, bis sie schier ausgebutzt waerre sin
darich die Verfolging.

Wo die Reformiering aagfange hot, scheint's hen die iwweriche Waldenser sich zu der Schweizerbrieder gschtellt, in
der Schweiz, Deitschland, un Holland. Viel vun der Fiehrer hen
der Mardierer-Dod glidde, so wie der Georg Blaurock, Felix
Manz, Michael Sattler, un viel annere. Der Menno Simons
(1496-1561) war endlich der Hauptfiehrer, weil er oft aus-
gwiche is, un is endlich en nadierlicher Dod gschterewe, deel
Yaahr dernooch.

Wann der glee Menno heem kummt vum Hoschbidaal, is en
Maad datt fer ihn griesse. Sell waar schunn ausgmacht en Paar
Monat vorher. Sie kann awwer yuscht zwee Woche bleiwe, dann
dien annere Maed aushelfe bis der Menno sex Woche alt is.

Fer die erschde paar Woche sin em Menno sei Gleeder
yuscht en Kutt un en Windel. Wann er vier Woche alt is, grickt
er en Frack aa am Blatz vun sei Kutt, en Unnerrock, un
schwatze Schtrimp. Sein Frack kummt nunner bis halbwegs

christening service. As a Mennonite, he will be baptized on faith after reaching the age of accountability. This is one of the tenets of faith that he inherits from Menno Simons.

Not that Menno Simons founded this faith. It was founded at the time of the apostles. Infant baptism was first practiced two hundred years later, at the time of Cyprian. During following centuries, infant baptism grew to such proportions that only a spark of the former faith remained. In the year 1160, Peter Waldo, of Lyons, France, revived baptism on confession of faith. For over a hundred years, the Waldensians flourished, only to be nearly crushed by persecution.

During the Reformation, some Waldensian survivors might have allied themselves with the Anabaptists or Swiss Brethren, as they were variously called, in Switzerland, Germany, and Holland. Many early leaders suffered a martyr's death, notably George Blaurock, Felix Manz, Michael Sattler, and many others. Menno Simons (1496-1561) became the accepted leader, partly because he evaded his captors to die a natural death years later.

When Baby Menno comes home from the hospital, a hired girl is there to greet him. Several months earlier, Menno's parents made arrangements for her service. However, she is only available for two weeks. Then other girls will leave their regular duties to help out until Menno is six weeks old.

For the first few weeks, Menno's clothes consist chiefly of a long flannelette nightgown and diapers. At four weeks of age, the nightie is replaced by a dress reaching halfway between knees and ankles, a pinafore, and black stockings. He wears dresses until he is about a year old. He never wears rompers or playsuits.

After the last hired girl leaves, Menno's mother is quite busy. She makes most of his clothes, besides doing the regular household chores. When Menno is peevish and fretful, as he some-

unnich die Gnie. Er waert en Frack bis er baut en Yaahr alt is. Er waert nie ken Rompers odder Schpielgleeder.

Wann die letscht Maad fattgeht, is em Menno sei Maem bissi. Sie macht es menscht vun seinre Gleeder, newich der gwehnlicher Hausaerwet. Wann der Menno griddlich is, wie er efters is, so hot sie ihre Hend voll; awwer sie beglaagt sich net. Der Menno is en Sege zu ihre, so macht sie es bescht davun.

Em Menno sei erschte Wadde sin net Englisch. Die Schprooch wo gschwetzt waet in sei Heemet is Pennsilfaani Deitsch, en Schprooch wo vun der Pfaltz, in Suddeitschland, kummt. Wiewohl es schunn ball dreihunnert Yaahre is das sie aus Europa kumme sin, hen die Mennischde ihre Mudderschprooch noch net verlore. Drum, bis der Menno in Schul geht, kann er zwee Schprooche schwetze.

Em Menno sei Maem helft melke mariyets un oweds, wann sie aa bissi is. Eb der Menno laafe kann, draagt sie ihn noch der Scheier, wo sie ihn in en leere Hammli Penn duht dieweil sie melkt. Er macht glei Freind mit der Katze, wo glei in die Penn neigraddele, fer gschmeechelt odder geblogt sei, so wie der Menno fiehlt.

Wann er mol elder is, brauch der Menno nimme gedraage sei. Er schpringt noch der Scheier mit em Hund hinnenooch, un dribbelt em Daed nooch wann er Vieh fiedert. Er watscht die Wutzlin suckle, un losst die Hammlin sei Hend schlotze. Der Buh un der Hund sin glei en gude Fuhr, un raessle un rolle minanner im Schtroh rum.

Eppes Neies kummt in em Menno sei Lewe wann er zwee Yaahre alt is; er grickt en gleene Schweschder. Nau is er nimme es eenzichscht wo sei Eldre sich drum bekimmere. Des erweckt zwee neie Gfiehle beim Menno: Lieb fer es Bobbi, un Missvergunscht fer die Lieb was die Eldre weise gehe's Bobbi. Die Maem browiert hatt fer es erscht uffbaue un es zwett demfe. Mit der Zeit gwinnt sie.

Weil der Menno ken ungwehnlich Kind is vun Naduur, halt er net lang ruhich. Im Summer schpielt er viel in der Sandbax.

times is, she has her hands full and is stressed. Yet she does not complain. She considers Menno to be a blessing and tries to make the best of things.

When Menno is old enough to talk, his first words are not English. The language spoken in his home, sometimes called Pennsylvania Dutch, is not Dutch at all, but a Palatinate German dialect. In this case, *Dutch/Deitsch* comes from *Deutsch* (German). Although it is almost three hundred years since they left Europe, the Mennonites have not lost their native tongue. When Menno enters school, he will also learn English and be truly bilingual.

Although Menno's mother is busy, she stills helps with the milking night and morning. Before Menno is old enough to walk, she carries him to the barn, where she puts him in an empty calf pen during milking time. He soon makes friends with the cats, who climb into the pen to be petted or tormented, depending on his whim.

As Menno grows older, he no longer needs to be carried. He runs to the barn, accompanied by the dog, to follow his father as he feeds the cattle. He watches the little pigs as they nurse, and lets the calves nuzzle his hands. Boy and dog become inseparable, frolicking and rolling over each other in the straw.

When Menno is two years old, a new element enters his life: a little sister. No longer is he the sole object of his parents' attention. Two new emotions awake in him—love for the baby and jealousy because of the affection bestowed upon her. His mother tries hard to cultivate the love and suppress the jealousy. As time wears on, his mother's efforts win.

Being a normal child, Menno never keeps still for long. In the summer, he often plays in the sandbox. It worries him not a bit that his toys are less expensive than those of most other children his age. His imagination creates a horse or a tractor out of the same spool or block of wood. At other times, he sits on the porch steps, alternately singing and kneeling, imitating what his people do in a church service.

Er is net bekimmert das er net so deier Schpielsach hot wie deel annere Kinner vun sei Elt. Er kann sich eibilde das en Holz-Glotz odder en Neez-Schpule en Gaul odder en Traekder is. Annere Mol sitzt er uff der Portschedreppe am singe, un dann am gniehe, so wie wann er in der Versammling waer.

Eb er in Schul geht, kimmert er sich nix das annere Kinner TV in ihre Heemet hen, odder das sie efter Kaendi, meh Schpielsach, un schennere Gleeder hen wie er. Er is zufridde, weil er es so gegwehnt is. Er beweist der Schpruch, "Genunk is was mer zufridde waer mit wann der Nochber net meh hett." Wann er dann un wann eppes Ungwehnliches grickt, is er werklich meh dankbaar davor wie die wo immer gucke fer so Sach, un nemme's fer ihre Deel.

Noch en Ursach das der Menno meh zufridde is, maag sei weil er laennt schaffe wann er yung is. Die menschde Mennischde Kinner hen leichte Hausaerwet zu duh eb sie in Schul gehn. Es is gaar net ungwehnlich as Vier-yaehriche Gscher abbutze, un ebmols aa wesche. Die Holzkischt fille, auskehre, un Bobbi hiede sin gwehnliche Gschefte fer die wo noch net in Schul gehn. Es hot aa Hammlin zu drenke, un Oier zu suche. Wann sie Deel vun der Zeit schaffe, waerre sie es Schpiele net so gschwind leedich.

Mennischde Kinner vun Schulelt kenne leicht verdeelt waerre in zwee Hauptgruppe: Die wo gern in Schul gehn, un die wo net dien. Bei die erscht Grupp is die Schul es Haupt vum Lewe. Wann sie Heem kumme owets sin ihre Haetze noch in Schul. Die Feierdaage sin gmesse bei die Leng Zeit bis die Schul widder schtert.

Die zwet Grupp is so viel annerscht wie die erscht as mieglich. Sie schicke sich fer Heem kumme noch der Schul, fer ausmischde, esse mache, bluge, odder Gaarde hacke. Sie losse sich ball net verschwetze fer en Buch uffmache daheem. Die Feierdaage sin Zeide fer zubringe in Scheier un Feld, Gaarde un Kich. Oh weh fer ennich-epper wo Schul benaamt an die Zeit!

Before Menno goes to school, he is not worried that other children have television in their homes or that they have frequent treats, more toys, and fancier clothes. Because he knows no other life, he is happy. This proves the proverb true: "Enough is what would satisfy us if our neighbor didn't have more." When Menno does receive a treat or a new plaything, he appreciates it more than do children who expect gifts regularly and take them for granted.

Another reason Menno is more content may be the fact that he learns to work at an early age. Most Mennonite children have light household chores to do before they reach school age. It is not uncommon for four-year-olds to dry dishes and occasionally wash them. Filling the woodbox, sweeping the floor, and minding the baby are common tasks for preschoolers. In the barn are calves to feed and eggs to gather. After spending some time in working, they are less apt to be bored by play.

School-aged Mennonite children can be divided into two main groups—those who like school and those who don't. For the former, school is the center around which life revolves. When they come home in the evening, their thoughts are still at school. Their summer holidays are measured by the number of days until school starts again.

Those of the second group are about as different from the first as possible. They hurry home after school to clean stables, prepare supper, plow a field, or hoe the garden. At home, they can hardly be persuaded to open a book. For them, the summer is a time to spend in barn or field, in garden or kitchen. During this time, woe to anyone who even mentions school!

Menno is one of the latter. He is not stupid. Menno could be a good pupil. But his love for the outdoors is too strong for him to enjoy being cooped up in a schoolhouse. His teacher finds it hard to arouse his interest in schoolwork. She recognizes a character worth developing, so she stimulates his interest in nature: birds, animals, trees, and flowers.

Though Menno does not care much for school, he does co-

Der Menno is eens vun der letschde Grupp. Er is wohl net dumm. Er kennt en guder Schuler sei; awwer sein Verlange fer draus sei is zu gross fer eigschpaett sei in der Schul. Sei Schulmiss hot en hadde Zeit fer ihn uffschtifde zu Schulaerwet. Doch seht sie das er eppes hot das dawaert is fer uffbaue; not browiert sie ihn eifrich griege wehe Veggel, Gediere, Baem, un Blumme.

Wiewohl as der Menno net viel gebt um die Schul, is er doch en aagenehmer Schuler, un will ken Druwwel mache. Was sei Eldre ihn laenne, halt ihn vun ungschickt zu sei. Schulaerwet is ihm ken Blessier, yuscht er duht es aus Schuldichkeit. Drum kann die Schulmiss sich uff ihn verlosse, so weit wie er es verschteht.

Der Menno is gscheftich vun Naduur, un brauchbaar beim Schpiele im Schulhof. Er is net vaddelhaftich. Wann die Schul aus is, macht er sich uff der Heemweg, un verseimt sich net. Alles iwwerhaupt zu nemme, findt die Schulmiss der Menno gut fer zweegkumme mit.

Schulhalde is ken leichde Sach fer sie. Mit ken hoche Laenning, hot sie ihre Hend voll mit dreissich Schuler in acht Klassen. Awwer sie beweist das gude Eigenschafde meh notwendich sin beim Schulhalde wie hoche Laenning. Sie schneit es Muschter fer gude Bauleit in der Gmee un in der Gsellschaft. Doch sorgt sie aa das die Schuler hielengliche Laenning griege das sie ihre eeges hewe kenne mit denne was in die Landschul gehn.

Der Menno geht net in Sunndaag-Schul. Sei Eldre glaawe, wie ihre Eldre aa hen, das wann sie ihre Schuldichkeit dien mit Kinner laenne daheem, not hot er genunk das er die Schrift alleenich unnersuche kann. Sie glaawe das es hot not net so viel Gfaahr das er sich selwer erhebt mit seiner Schrift-Laenning. Er hot sei eeye Biewel-Gschichde Buch, un en Nei Teschdament, wo sei Maem ihm rausleest bis er selwer lese kann.

Wo der Menno noch en Bobbi waar, hen sei Eldre ihn mit in die Versammling gnumme in em uffeniche Boggi, un sei Maem

operate, unlike some others who make trouble. His parents' teaching holds him back from gross disobedience. He does not deliberately cause trouble. His schoolwork is not a pleasure to him, but he accepts it as a duty. Therefore, the teacher can depend on him to do his assignments according to his ability.

Menno is active by nature and puts enthusiastic effort into the games on the playground. Here, too, the teacher finds him dependable and not inclined to take advantage of others. Then, after school closes in midafternoon, he is on his way home as soon as possible, without loitering. Taking these facts into consideration, the teacher does not find it difficult to appreciate Menno as a pupil.

The teacher has undertaken a huge task. With no more than an eighth-grade education, she needs to give all she has to be able to teach thirty pupils in eight grades. Yet she has proved that for a teacher, there are more important qualifications than a good education. She casts the mold for future citizens, supplying them with an education that shows up well alongside what is taught in public schools.

Menno does not go to Sunday school. His parents believe, as did their parents before them, that if they do their duty by teaching him at home, he will eventually have enough training to be able to study the Scriptures himself. That way, they believe he is less likely to pride himself in his churchly accomplishments. He has a Bible story book of his own, as well as a New Testament, from which his mother reads to him until he is able to read by himself.

When Menno is a baby, his parents take him to meeting in the open buggy, which has one seat; his mother holds him on her lap. Later, he sits on the little seat in the buggy box, with his back to the dashboard. In the meetinghouse, he sits with his father, usually on the second bench from the front, close to the men's door. After he has gone to school for a few years, he is allowed to sit with the boys on one of the front benches facing the ministry.

hot ihn uff der Schoos ghowe. Schpeeder sitzt er uff em gleene Sitzli vanne in der Boggibax, un bei seim Daed in der Versammling. Sie sitze gwehnlich uff der zwetveddersch Bank naegscht bei der Mennerdaer. Nochdem er en Paar Yaahre in Schul gange is, daerf er bei der gleene Buwe sitze, uff eens vun der zwee vedderschde Benk, naegscht bei dem Breddichschtul. Bis des Zeit sin noch mehner Kinner in der Famillye, so das es Boggi nimme gross genunk is. Em Menno sein Daed kaaft yetzt en Zweegeilskaritsch, mit Sitz fer rumschiewe. So weit brauche sie yuscht noch zwee Sitz. Wann es noch meh Blatz braucht, kenne sie der hinnerscht Sitz noch weider zerick schiewe, un noch en gleene Sitz zwischenei duh. Not sin der zwett un der dritt Sitz geyenanner gedreht.

Gwehnlich waert der Menno en wennich uffgregt Sunndaag-Mariyets. Wann Versammling is in Nadd Woolwich, not fangt es Rischdes schunn Freidaags aa, mit Backes vun allehand, fer Bsuch. Ebmols, wann der Menno an der rechde Zeit in die Kich kummt, kann er en gedreelder Kuche griege zum versuche. Samschdaags is als Butzes zu duh im Haus un in der Scheier. Die Schtell misse all ausgmischt waerre, so das wennicher Aerwet is am Sunndaag-Mariye.

Wann der Menno wacker waert, is der Daed schunn in der Scheier am rischde fer melke. Der Menno dummelt sich fer die Hammlin drenke un Hoi gewwe. Wann er um der Weg is, gebt's alsemols en Gleyeheit fer en nei Gscheft griege. Ball is es Zeit fer Mariye-Esse. Es hot Corn Flakes un Millich mit Aebeere, im Blatz vun Hawwermosch wie gwehnlich, weil sell net so viel Zeit nemmt fer rischde.

Noch em Esse muss der Menno Hals un Ohre wesche, wo er net gern duht. Sein Daed butzt die Geil un gschaett sie uff, eb er neikummt fer sich rumschtrippe. Not muss die Deck nausgnumme waerre uff die Karitsch, un die Gleene all eigebundelt. Der Menno sitzt uff em vedderschde Sitz newich em Daed, dann sin sie reddi fer geh.

Es nemmt net lang fer die vier Meil faahre zu der Versamm-

As time passes, there are more children in the family, so the open buggy is no longer large enough. Menno's father buys a carriage with movable seats. First, only two seats are needed. If more room is needed later, the rear seat can be moved back and a third seat placed backward against the back of the front seat.

Menno generally becomes slightly excited when Sunday comes. If there is a meeting at North Woolwich, preparations start on Friday, with baking of all kinds for the expected visitors. He likes to slip into the kitchen for a sample cookie. On Saturday there is cleaning to do in house and barn, in preparation for possible visitors.

When Menno wakes up, his father is already at the barn, getting ready to milk. Menno hurries to feed the calves with milk and hay. There is always the chance that if he sticks around, he may be entrusted with a new job. Soon it is time for breakfast: cornflakes, milk, and strawberries instead of the usual oatmeal porridge, to save time.

After breakfast, Menno has to wash his neck and ears, a job he does not relish. His father grooms and harnesses the team before he washes up and changes into his Sunday clothes. Then they take blankets out to the carriage and bundle in the smaller children. Menno sits on the front seat with his father, and they are ready to start.

Soon they cover the four miles, and Menno can see the meetinghouse. It is a modest long, low building, almost like an army barracks, about fifty by seventy feet. Some of the older meetinghouses are frame buildings with white clapboard siding, but this one is built of white brick. All the outside woodwork is painted white, and the roof is green.

Along the road to the east of the meetinghouse lies the cemetery, with its rows of plain white tombstones. On every side of the meetinghouse are rows of posts with heavy chains strung over the top, where the horses are tied. Menno can already see many horses tied, some wearing horse blankets while others

ling, un ball seht der Menno es Versammlinghaus. Es is yuscht
en eefach, lang, nidder Gebei, fuffzich bei siwwezich Fuuss.
Deel vun der alde Heiser warre vun weiss Glabbord gmacht,
awwer des is weiss backeschtehnich. Es eisserscht Holzwerk is
alles weiss, un es Dach is grien.

Em Weg nooch, oscht vum Versammlinghaus, is der Graab-
hof, mit Roihe vun weisse Graabschtee. Uff alle Seide vum Haus
sin Roihe vun Poschde mit schwere Kedde owwedriwwer, wo
die Geil aagebunne waerre. Der Menno seht schunn etliche
Geil aagebunne: en Deel zugedeckt, un annere noch net. Es
Wedder is schee, so es mechde ball zwee hunnert Geil do aagebunne sei bis die Versammling aageht.

Der Daed faahrt die Karitsch newe an die Portsch, wo die
voll Leng vun em Oschtend herlaaft. Die Maem geht runner
mit der zwee glennschde Kinner, zu der middelscht Schtiwwli-
Daer nei. Datt sin Schelfer fer die Bannets, un Hoke fer die
Schaals un Kiddels. Datt bsucht sie mit annere Weibsleit
dieweil sie die Kinner ausziegt.

Der Menno binnt der eent Gaul an die Kett, dieweil der Daed
der anner aabinnt un sie zudeckt. Der Menno schmeisst sein
Iwwerrock uff der Sitz, un geht mit der annere gleene Buwe zu
der Daer nei gehe der Weg, un setzt sich uff die vedderscht
Bank uff der rechtze Seit; die Maed sitze uff die links Seit.

Vun seim Sitz uff der vedderscht Bank kann der Menno gut
iwwer die ganz Schtubb sehne. Die gebleschdert Wand is weiss,
awwer es Holzwerk is gaar net aagschtriche. Der Breddichschtul schteht uff die Mitt vun der sudd Wand, graad gehe der
Menno gedreht. Die Daer wo die Menner rei-kumme is in der
Mitt vun em wescht Giwwelend. Die Benk uff der nadd Seit
vun der Daer sin all gehe Sudde gedreht. Die alde Weiwer sitze
am annere End, un gucke Wescht. Die Diener sitze hinnich em
Breddichschtul un gucke Nadde. Holziche Hiet-Raecks henke
vun owwerunner owwich der Mannsleit.

Zwee Breddicher un een Eldeschde kumme der Mannsleit-
Daer rei ungfaehr zehe Minudde eb's Zeit is fer aafange, un

are just being covered. Since the weather is fair, there may be nearly two hundred horses tied to the chains by the time the meeting is ready to start.

The carriage pulls up alongside the porch, which runs the full length of the east gable end. Here Menno's mother gets off with the two smallest children. She enters the center cloakroom door, where there are shelves for the bonnets and hooks for shawls and coats. As she unwraps her little ones, she visits with the other women.

Menno ties one of the horses to the chain, while his father ties the other one and straps their blankets on. Leaving his overcoat on the carriage seat, Menno starts toward the meetinghouse with the other boys of his age. They enter the door that faces the road and sit on one of the two front benches facing the ministers. The benches to the left are for the girls and are taboo for the boys.

From his seat on the front bench, Menno commands a good view of the room before him. The plastered walls are white, but none of the woodwork is painted. The pulpit stands along the center of the south wall, so Menno is almost directly in front of it. The door by which the men enter is in the center of the west gable end. All the benches on the north side of this door face south and are occupied by the young people and the

En Mennischde Versammlinghaus
A Typical Mennonite Meetinghouse

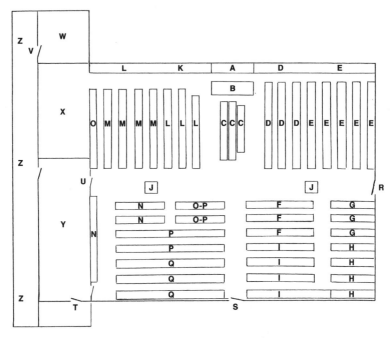

Ausleging der Versammling
Key to Meetinghouse Layout

A Diener/ministry
B Breddichschtul/pulpit
C Benk fer naus-schtelle/spare benches
D alde Menner/older men
E middelalde Menner/middle-aged men
F yunge Buwe/boys
G yunggheierde Menner/newly married men
H Menner mit Kinner/young married men with children
I grosse Buwe/older boys
J Hitzoffe/oil heaters
K Dieners Weiwer/wives of ministers
L alde Weiwer/older women
M middelalde Weiwer/middle-aged women
N Weiwer mit Kinner/mothers with children

O yunggheierde Weiwer/newly married women
P gleene Meed/young girls
Q grosse Meed/older girls
R Menner Daer/men's entrance
S Buwe Daer/boys' entrance
T Meed Daer/girls' entrance
U yunge Weiwer Daer/young women's entrance
V alde Weiwer Daer/older women's entrance
W Weibsleit Heisli/women's washrooms
X alde Weiwer Schtiwwli un Rot Kemmerli/older women's cloakroom, and counsel room
Y yunge Weibsleit Schtiwwli/younger women's cloakroom
Z Portsch/loading porch

newly married, with young men on the west side and young women on the east.

The benches for the older men face east and are south of the men's door. The older women sit at the opposite end, facing west. The *Diener* (servants, ministers) sit behind the wide pulpit, facing north. Wooden hat racks are suspended from the ceiling over the men's and boy's sections.

A preacher and a deacon have been ordained for each meetinghouse. But since services alternate between meetinghouses, a minister who is free usually attends a meeting at another place. When he does, he is expected to take part in the service. At the beginning of the service, the home preacher offers the pulpit Bible to the visiting minister, who usually delivers the main sermon. Any visiting deacon would be invited to read the text.

About ten minutes before the 10:00 a.m. meeting time, the two preachers and one deacon enter the men's door and take their place behind the pulpit. As they pass through the room, they shake hands with the old men on the front bench.

Unless there is a specific reason to do otherwise, all services are conducted in German. At the right time, the home preacher or deacon announces a hymn and reads the first verse. One of the two song leaders starts the hymn, singing the first syllable of each verse alone. After that, the whole congregation joins in, singing with a slow rhythm. The hymns have an average of about eight verses, and the people usually sing them through to the end.

When the first hymn is finished, the visiting deacon reads from the New Testament a chapter selected by the main speaker. After he is finished, the home preacher delivers an opening sermon, about a half hour in length. He bases his message on no particular text but attempts to open the hearts of the congregation for the main sermon. As he finishes, the congregation kneels for a short silent prayer.

After the prayer, the visiting preacher delivers the main ser-

nemme ihre Bletz hinnich em Breddichschtul. Wann sie an der
vedderscht Bank verbei gehn, gewwe sie der Daadis wo datt
sitze "Wie gehts." Es hot een Breddicher un een Eldeschter fer
yedes Versammlinghaus; yuscht weil net an yedem Haus Versammling is yeden Sunndaag, kumme die wo ken Heem-Ver-
sammling hen not an eens von der annere Bletz in Versammling un nemme gwehnlich Deel. Wann die Versammling aafangt,
hebt der Heemdiener em annere Breddicher die Biewel anne,
wo dann die Hauptbreddich bringt.

Wann ken Ursach is fer net, is alles Deitsch. Wann es Zeit is
fer aafange, gebt der Heembreddicher odder Eldeschder en
Lied aus, un lest der erscht Vaersch ab. Eens vun der zwee
Vorsinger fangt es Lied aa, un singt die erscht Not vun yedem
Vaersch alleenich. Dann helfe die annere Leit all, mit en
langsame Tackmeesichkeit. Die menschde Lieder hen ungfaehr
acht Vaersch, un sie waerre gwehnlich all gsunge.

Wann es Lied faddich gsunge is, lest een Eldeschder en
Schtick Schrift ab, wo erwaehlt is waerre vun em Breddicher
wo es Hauptdeel nemmt: der Text wo er erwaehlt hot. Dann
macht der Heemdiener en Eigang vun verleicht en halb
Schtund. Er hot ken Text, awwer browiert fer die Haetze uffmache zu der Schrift. Dann gniet die ganz Versammling fer en
ruhich Gebet.

Noch dem Gebet schteht der Bsuch Breddicher uff, un breddicht vun em abglesener Text. Er hot nix abgschriwwe, un
breddicht yuscht wie der Geischt ihn fiehrt. Nadierlich, die
nehmlich Graft wo gebraucht waar fer die Schrift schreiwe is
alsnoch dabei fer die Breddich fiehre.

Am End vun der Breddich gewwe die iwweriche Diener noch
Zeignis zu der Breddich. Dann gniet die Versammling, un der
Breddicher, wo gschtanne hot, fiehrt en laut Gebet. Dann
waert noch en Lied gsunge, der Sege gschproche, un die Versammling zum Schluss gebrocht.

Em Menno sei Maem un Daed laade gwehnlich Bsuch ei vun
annere Bezirke fer Middaag odder Nachtesse. Der Menno is

mon, based on the whole chapter read by the deacon. He may have studied the text the day before, but more likely not, since he does not know before that morning whether he is expected to preach on the text. He uses no notes or helps but talks as the Spirit leads him. After all, the same God who inspired the Scriptures to be written is still available to inspire the sermon.

At the close of the sermon, the ministers who had no leading part in the service testify to its truth. Then the congregation kneels while the main speaker leads in audible prayer. At the close of the prayer, the second song leader announces a hymn, which is followed by the benediction and any announcements, and the meeting is over.

Menno's father and mother usually invite visitors from other church districts who happen to be in the meeting to come to their house for dinner (noon) or supper. Menno is eager to know whether anyone is coming. When the answer is yes, he wants to know whether the visiting family has any boys his age. There is one, so Menno is happy. Having company his age on Sunday is the highlight of his week.

When there is company, Sunday dinner is a treat in itself. A typical dinner offers homemade bread, butter and jam, mashed potatoes, pork sausage and gravy, canned peas, pickles, canned peaches, cookies, and pie. Menno is glad that when company is present, no one stops a boy who takes larger helpings than usual.

Before dinner, the boys don't get started playing. They check each other's age and school grade. During the meal, they are expected to keep quiet and eat. After dinner, a neighbor boy comes over, and the playing starts in earnest. Upstairs in the barn, they play bag tick and hide-and-seek. They swap stories of big tractors and fast horses. When four o'clock comes and the visitors leave, they are not ready to quit.

On a Sunday when there is no meeting at North Woolwich, the pattern is slightly different. There is less cleaning and baking in preparation for Sunday. Instead, more effort is put into

gwunnerich wer kumme kennt. Wann er heert das Bsuch
kummt, wunnert er eb sie Buwe hen vun sei Elt. Sie hen eener,
un der Menno is froh. Bsuch uff der Sunndaag is die greescht
Blessier vun der Woch.

Sunndaag-Middaag, wann's Bsuch hot, is schunn en Blessier
in sich selwer. Dann hot's efters heemgmacht Brot, Budder un
Schmieres, gschtammde Grummbeere, Brotwaescht un Brieh,
Erbse, Pickels, Paesching, Kuche, un Pei. Sell is net all; awwer
wann es Bsuch hot, dann nemmt niemand in Acht wann mer
mehner esst!

Die Buwe griege net gschtaert Schpiele vor dem Esse. Sie
froge enanner wehe ihre Elt, un wie weit sie sin in der Schul.
Dieweil gesse waet, is geguckt davor das sie ruhich sin un esse.
Noch em Middaag, wann eens vun der Nochber's Buwe
kummt, geht's los in Ernscht. Owwer in der Scheier schpiele sie
Sack Tick un Verschteckle. Sie verzehle Schtories vun grosse
Traekders un schnelle Geil. Wann es vier Uhr is, un Zeit fer
Heem geh, sin sie noch gaar net faeddich.

Uff en Sunndaag wo ken Nadd Woolwich Versammling is,
geht es en wennich annerscht her. Es hot wenniger Butzes un
Backes zu duh, awwer die Gleeder un Fuhrwerke misse reddi
sei fer weiter faahre. Die Aerwet muss frieher geduh sei wann
es zwelf Meil is zu faahre.

Desemol sin ken Buwe fer der Menno mitschpiele, weil sie
eldre Leit bsuche. Der Menno find es doch indressant. Die
Mannsleit iwwerhole Gmee Gschichde, un der Menno is ganz
eignumme mit der Schtories. Sie schwetze vun der Zeit vier
hunnert Yaahre zerick, wo die Schweizerbrieder verfolgt un
gemaerdert waerre sin wehe ihrem Glaawe. Viel vun ihne sin
gflicht noch der Pfalz un noch Holland. Datt hen sie im Friede
lewe kenne, awwer sie waare aarm un verschtoose.

Darich der Quaker, Wilhelm Penn, hen sie dann en Land
gfunne vun Millich un Hunnich iwwer der See, in Pennsilfaani,
zwischich 1710 un 1730, wo sie dann en schtarke Gmee
gebaut hen in en fremm Land.

preparing clothes and equipment for a longer trip. The chores need to be done earlier, to give them time for a twelve-mile drive.

This time the family is visiting older people, and there are no boys for Menno to play with. However, he finds it interesting all the same. The men discuss church history, and Menno is absorbed in the stories.

They talk about the time four hundred years ago when the Swiss Brethren were persecuted and martyred for their faith. Many of them fled to the Palatinate, and some to Holland. There they could live in peace, but they suffered from poverty and crowded conditions. Through the benevolence of William Penn, they found their land of milk and honey beyond the ocean. From 1710 to 1730, hundreds found refuge in Pennsylvania, where they established a strong Mennonite colony.

Suddenly Menno realizes with a shock that he is listening to history and enjoying it! It is more interesting when the history is about people like himself. He is fascinated by the story of the group of hardy pioneers who moved to new lands again, this time to the wilds of Upper Canada, now Ontario. Those who settled in Woolwich Township came between 1820 and 1830. Here they started a new life, building their homes with logs they cleared off the land.

The men talk on. Some of the Mennonites built towns with shops, hotels, and breweries. It became clear that the church was suffering from the prosperity of the people. Some Mennonites worried that their people were not dressed as simply as before. They were copying more of the world's ways, instead of remaining *separate and peculiar*.

Other Mennonites, such as those from around Berlin (Kitchener) and farther south, thought the answer would be in Sunday schools and prayer meetings. Woolwich Township was the stronghold of the Old Orders, who rejected such new practices. In 1889 the two groups divided, with the Woolwich Old Orders retaining about a third of the total membership.

Uff emol is der Menno wacke waerre. Er is am hariche zu Hischtorie un is vergniegt dabei! Er findt's viel meh blessierlich wann es vun Leit is wie er selwer. Er is ganz eignumme mit der Grupp unverzaagte Weg-baahner wo widder noch en nei Land gezogge sin; desemol noch Kanadaa. Die wo sich in Woolwich daheem gmacht hen sin kumme zwische 1820 un 1830. Datt hen sie en nei Lewe aagfange, in Blockheiser, gmacht vun der Baem wo sie vun ihrem Land ghackt hen.

Die Mannsleit sin alsnoch em verzaehle. En Deel vun der Mennischde hen Schteddel gebaut, mit Schapps, Waettsheiser, un Brauereie. Es hot gscheint wie wann die Gmee hinnerschich gange waer, weil es der Leit zu gut gange is. Deel vun der Men- nischde hen Hochmut gedriwwe. Sie hen der Welt ihre Wege noochgmacht, not waare sie nimme *bei sich selwer un ungwehnlich*.

Deel hen gmehnt es brauch Sunndaag-Schule un Bet- schtunde. Die wo neecher bei der grosse Schtedt waare, bei Kitchener, hen's schtaeriker dreiwe welle. In 1889 hen die zwee Gruppe sich verdeelt. Die Altmodische vun Woolwich hen um en Drittel vun der Leit ghalde.

In 1939 waar noch en Verdeeling. Deel vun der Leit hen Kars un Foons welle, un doch die iwweriche alde Addninge halde. Selle hen sich zu der Gmee gschtellt an Markham, wo schunn am Kars faahre waare. Sell is nau die Waterloo- Markham Gmee, un hen net ganz die Helft vun der Gmee mit- gnumme. Es hot noch meh gleene Deelinge gewwe, awwer net das viel uff sich ghat hen.

Der Menno is dief in der Gedanke uff em Heemweg: Wie waer es fer zu der Markham Gmee gheere? Odder, wie waer es fer bei der Unnere sei, bei Kitchener? Er schemmt sich ball fer denke davun. Er glaabt es waer doch schendlich fer farewiche Kars faahre, TV hawwe, un alles schunscht was mir denke kennt davun, un dann in Sunndaag-Schul geh, un alsnoch en Mennischt sei. Sell dinkt ihn net wie der Mennischde Glaawe an Demut.

In 1939 another major division occurred. Some Old Order Mennonites wished to have cars and telephones, and still keep the other customs and doctrines the same. These associated themselves with the church at Markham, whose members already drove cars. This group became known as the Markham Mennonites; they carried about 40 percent of the Old Order membership with them.

Many smaller divisions occurred among the Mennonites, but most did not affect the Old Order church as deeply as the ones of 1889 and 1939.

On the way home, Menno is deep in thought: What would it be like to belong to the Markham church? Or to live among the liberal Mennonites? Just the thought gives him a feeling of guilt. Menno does not understand how people can ride in brightly colored cars, have television, and own almost everything else the world offers—and then go to Sunday school and still claim to be Mennonite. That doesn't seem to him like true faith and obedience.

Die Alt-Mennischde sin gekennt bei ihre eefache Gleeder. Doh sin Pickders vun ihre Gleeder wo sie rausschteh mache vun der iwweriche Leit vun der Welt.

The Old Order Mennonites are recognized by their plain clothing. Here are sketches of articles of clothing that distinguish them from the world outside their group.

Latzhosse, fer Diener un alde Mann-
sleit/broadfall pants, for ministers
and older men, with the plain coat
and vest, for a dress suit

Kaep Iwwerrock, wo die Diener
waere/cape overcoat, worn by
the ministers

Tschaecket/plain vest

Mutze/plain coat

Menno is wondering about life in those earlier times: What if he had to live in a log cabin in the woods and carry all the water from a spring, like the early pioneers? What if he had lived in Europe and gone to a meeting on a dark rainy night, hidden somewhere in the woods for fear of the Anabaptist hunters? He shudders at the thought. Yet, according to the visiting this afternoon, the church then was stronger than at any time since.

Weiwer Summer Bannet/women's summer bonnet

Weiwer Winder Bannet/women's winter bonnet

Mannsleit Winde Kapp/men's winter cap

Mannsleit Sundaags Hut/ men's Sunday hat

Der Menno denkt aa vun der friehe Baahnbrecher ihrem Lewe: Was waer es gleich gwesst fer in en Blockhaus im Busch wohne, un es Wasser heemdraage vun der Schpring? Odder wie waer es fer in Versammling geh im Dunkle, bei Reggewedder, verschluppt im Busch, wehe verfolgt waerre? Es schaudert der Menno; doch, wie sie gschwetzt hen der Nochmiddaag, hot die Gmee mehner zugnumme sell Zeit wie an enniche annere Zeit.

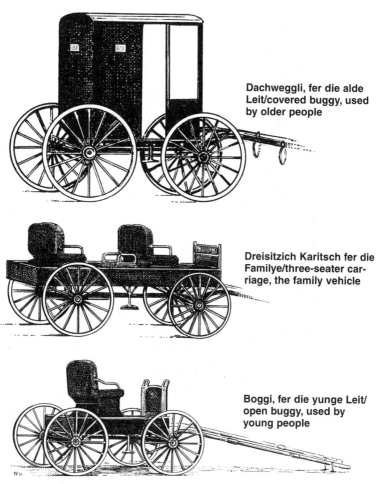

Dachweggli, fer die alde Leit/covered buggy, used by older people

Dreisitzich Karitsch fer die Familye/three-seater carriage, the family vehicle

Boggi, fer die yunge Leit/ open buggy, used by young people

Weibsleit Frack, Schaets, un Kaep/women's three-piece outfit: dress, apron, and cape (back view)

Bibschaetz, wie die Meed waere/bib apron, worn by girls while working

Weibsleit Kapp/women's cap, prayer covering

Weibsleit Schaal/women's shawl

Beim uffwaxe

WANN DER MENNO vaetzeh waet, is es nimme geguckt davor das er noch in Schul geht. Er fiehlt wie wann er yetzt gross waer. Er kann der ganz Daag im Feld schaffe, mit em Traekder odder der Fuhr. Er schafft net fatt, weil er noch sei Laenning daheem uff der Bauerei grickt. Die Schul-Amtsleit gewwe ihm es Recht fer aus der Schul bleiwe an der vaetzeh, wann er sei Laenning aahalt daheem an der Bauere-aerwet.

Sell is aa die Zeit wo er aafangt sich en wennich vermenge mit der Yunge. Er is noch zu yung fer an Singings geh, awwer er daerf uffbleiwe wann en Singing bei ihne daheem is. Er guckt vaerre halwe im Zweifel, halwe mit Gluschde, zu der Zeit wann sell vorkumme mecht.

Endlich glappts. Uff em Heemweg vun der Versammling macht der Daed en Aamerking das eens vun der grosse Buwe ihn gfrogt hot wehe en Singing hawwe.

"Was hoscht ihm gsaat?" frogt die Maem.

"Ich hab gsaat ich geb nix drum, wann es dir nix ausmacht."

"Ya, well"—der Menno hebt sein Odem bis die Maem antwatt. "Ich hab en Deel gebacke, awwer ich wees net eb es genunk is. Ich kennt noch Jello mache. Es Weschhaus is woll net arig sauwer."

"Ich kann es Weschhaus auskehre," biet der Menno aa.

"Ich glaab net das sie viel gucke wie es Weschhaus guckt," mehnt der Daed. "Ennichweg, sie brauche gaar net in es Weschhaus geh. Es waer mir liewer wann sie net deede."

Mit sellem dreibt der Daed die Geil en wennich, un der Menno glaabt es is ausgmacht.

Growing Up

WHEN MENNO reaches the age of fourteen, he is no longer expected to go to school. He has the feeling of being grown-up, since now he can work all day in the fields, driving the tractor or a team of horses. He does not leave home to work because he is officially apprenticed to Father. The government authorities grant him permission to leave school at fourteen if he continues his education at home. This he accomplishes by learning farmwork.

At fourteen, Menno also begins to enter the grown-up world socially. He is not old enough to go to the youth singings, but he is allowed to stay up when there is a singing at his home. He looks forward with mixed anticipation and apprehension to the Sunday when this takes place.

At last, he is rewarded. On the way home from meeting, Father casually observes, "One of the boys asked me about having a singing at our place."

"What did you tell him?" Mother asks.

"I said I won't mind, if you agree."

"Well,"—Menno listens with bated breath for Mother's answer—"we did some baking, but I don't know whether there will be enough. I could soon prepare some Jell-O. The washhouse is not very clean, though."

"I can sweep the washhouse," volunteers Menno.

"I guess they won't worry much how the washhouse looks," Father says. "Anyway, they don't need to go into the washhouse. I wish they wouldn't."

With this final remark, Father urges the horses on, and Menno considers the matter settled.

Um finf Uhr faahre zwee Boggis nei. All zwee sin Buwe en wennich elder wie der Menno. Wann sie die Geil im Schtall hen, nemmt der Menno sie nei in die Schtubb, un duht es Krokinol Bord uff der Fliegeldisch. Dann geht er naus an sei Owedaerwet wann die Buwe aafange schpiele. An der Kiehschtalldaer drefft er der Daed aa.

"Es guckt net wie wann viel kumme deede fer es Nachtesse," mehnt der Menno.

"Ich hab net gedenkt das es dien," antwatt der Daed, "weil du noch net an Singing gehscht. Sell is worum ich gedenkt hab es kennt geh wann die Maem aa nix vannenaus gwisst hot davun."

Um die acht Uhr fange noch mehner Boggis aa kumme. Der Menno helft der Erschde ausschpanne un die Geil in der Schtall duh, not gehn sie noch em Haus un losse die iwweriche ihre Geil alleenich weckduh. Der Menno is bekimmert das er neikummt fer helfe singe, weil er net oft die Geleyeheit hot fer singe mit en Drupp. Sie singe aus der *Christian Hymnal* Bicher. Weil em Menno sei Schtimm sich noch net faddich verennert hot, singt er Soprano. Es menscht vun der Buwe singe Tenor odder Bass.

Um die zehe Uhr heert der Menno en Uffruhr im Weschhaus. Gwunnerich was am geh is, geht er an die Daer. Der Disch is newenaus gschowe. Een Buh is am Maulmusick schpiele, un etliche annere zwerwele uff em Bodde rum. Der Menno mehnt sie misste daermlich waerre.

Uff eemol gschpiert er en Hand uff sei Schulder, wo ihn sanft newenaus schiebt. Dann heert er em Daed sei Schtimm.

"Es duht mir Leed, Buwe, awwer es waer mir liewer wann dir eppes schunscht duh deedet. Ich bin froh wann dir eich vergnieyet, awwer ich will ken Maulmusick Schpieles un Danzes in meim Haus. Dir kennet gewiss eppes schunscht finne fer duh."

Etliche vun der Buwe grummele en wennich unnich ihrem Odem. Paar vun ihne gucke en wennich verzaagt. Niemand saagt

About five o'clock, two buggies arrive. Both are boys only a few years older than Menno. When the horses are stabled, he takes the boys into the living room and sets the crokinole board on the dropleaf table. As the visiting boys begin to play, he hurries out to do his chores. At the cow stable door, he meets his father.

"It doesn't look as if there will be many coming for supper," Menno remarks.

"I didn't expect there would be," Father replies, "since you don't go to singing yet. That's why I thought it would be all right to let them come, even if Mother didn't know about it earlier."

At about eight o'clock, more buggies start coming. Menno helps these new arrivals to unhitch and stable their horses. Then they all head for the house, leaving the youth coming later to stable their horses for themselves. Menno is eager to get in and help with the singing, since he seldom has the chance to sing in harmony with a group. They are using the *Christian Hymnal*. Since Menno's voice has not fully developed, he sings soprano. Most of the boys sing tenor or bass.

At about ten o'clock, Menno hears a commotion in the washhouse. He goes to the door, curious to see what is going on. The table has been pushed aside. One boy is playing a mouth organ and several others are whirling around on the floor. Menno thinks they must surely be growing dizzy.

Suddenly he feels a hand on his shoulder, gently pushing him aside. Then he hears Father's voice beside him.

"I'm sorry, boys, but I would rather have you do something else. I like to see you enjoying yourselves, but I don't want mouth organ playing and dancing in my house. Surely you can find something else to do."

Several of the boys grumble under their breath. Others look sheepish. No one speaks. Gradually they drift back into the kitchen, where sitting games are now in process.

So that is dancing, Menno thinks.

eppes. Endlich gehn sie langsam nei in die Kich wo Sitz-
Gschpiel am geh is.

So sell is Danzes, denkt der Menno.

Die eldere Buwe gehn not fer ihre Maed heemfaahre. Die
Iwweriche dien noch en Weil Zeit neibemble, so halbleinich
am schpiele. Es is Mittnacht bis die Letschde fattgehn, un der
Menno in es Bett geht.

Der Menno geht net an der See im Sommer, odder Haesch-
yaage im Winder. Er maecht velleicht emol an der Fall geh,
odder zu der Dausend Eilands. Doch Blessierfaahres is im
ganzem net fer es Bescht aagsehne.

Es hot woll ee Satt Reeses wo der Menno einemme kennt, un
wo er vaerre guckt dezu wann er emol alt genunk is—fer
Freind bsuche in der Schteets. Sei Eldre maechte sogaar selwer
so en Rees nemme.

Lengeschder Kaundi, Pennsilfaani, is die Gegend vun wo die
Mennischde doher kumme sin. Es waare aa schunn ee hunnert
Yaahre Mennischde in Virginia un Indiana, awwer die Gegen-
der waare net so gross. In der letschde fuffzich Yaahre is die
Lengeschder Gmee so gross gwaxe das sie mehner Blatz
brauche. Yetzt sin neie Kolonies in Berks, Union, Blair, un
Cumberland Kaundies in Pennsilfaani, un in Nei Yarick, Ohio,
Wisconsin, Missouri, un Kentucky.

Wann der Daed mol en Aamerking macht wann er heem
kummt vum Schteddel, wehe uff en Rees geh, is der Menno
verleicht mehner uffgregt wie die Maem.

"Es Levis welle naegscht Woch noch Pennsilfaani geh, un
hen gwunnert eb mir mitgeh deede. Nadierlich kenne mir net."

"Ferwas net?" frogt der Menno. "Ich kann die Aerwet
schaffe."

"Wie lang welle sie bleiwe?" frogt die Maem.

"Baut zehe Daag."

"Wann mer epper griege kennt fer aushelfe—denkscht die

The older boys are now leaving to take their girlfriends home. The rest fool around a little longer, halfheartedly playing games. At midnight the last ones leave, and Menno goes to bed.

Menno does not go to the beach in the summer or to a hunting camp in the winter. Sometime he might go to see Niagara Falls, the Thousand Islands, or some other natural wonder. In general, pleasure trips are looked upon with disapproval. However, Menno may indulge in one type of travel, and he looks forward to enjoying it when he reaches a suitable age. He would like to visit friends in a distant country. In fact, his parents might take such a trip.

Lancaster County, Pennsylvania, is the mother colony of the Mennonites. There have also been settlements in Virginia and Indiana for over a hundred years, but those are comparatively small. In the past fifty years, the Lancaster community has grown to such proportions that farmland became too expensive and expansion was urgent. As a result, new settlements have sprung up in Berks, Union, Blair, and Cumberland counties in Pennsylvania, and in New York, Ohio, Wisconsin, Missouri, and Kentucky.

When Father returns from town and makes a casual remark about a trip, Menno is likely more excited than Mother.

"Levis want to go to Pennsylvania next week and asked if we would go along. Of course, we can't go."

"Why can't you go?" Menno questions. "I can do the work."

"How long do they plan to stay?" Mother asks.

"About ten days."

"If we could get someone to help out—do you think we could get Anna for a few days?"

"Perhaps. And someone to help Menno—"

"I can get along," Menno insists. He actually looks forward to doing the work alone.

Finally, it is decided Menno's parents will go along to Penn-

Anna kennt en Paar Daag kumme?" wunnert die Maem.

"Verleicht; un epper fer em Menno helfe—"

"Ich kumm zweeg," sagt der Menno. Er guckt werklich vaerre dazu.

Endlich is es ausgmacht das sie gehn, wann die Anna kummt fer haushalde, un der Nochber Paul als widder guckt eb der Menno Hilf braucht.

"Es is werklich net viel das graad yetzt geduh sei muss," mehnt der Daed endlich. "Du kannscht Mischt faahre, un am Samschdaag kenne die Kinner helfe Schtee leese. Geb Acht das die Kieh net uffbleehe, weil sie uff frische Weed sin. Wann es Druwwel gebt, saag's em Paul. Er kann dir saage eb du der Geilsdokder griege settscht."

"Brauchscht dich net baddere," mehnt der Menno widder. "Mir kumme zweeg."

Em Menno sei Eldre sin noch net viel greest sidder das sie gheiert hen, so es hot viel zu sehne. Sie verstaune sich iwwer der Burlington Skyway, Lake Ontario, un der Welland Kanaal. Sie griege yuscht en Blick vun em Niagara Fall, awwer sie waerre doch eifrich fer denke das sie so naegscht dabei sin. An Buffalo gehn sie iwwer die Grenze, un griege der erscht Blick vun der Schteets.

Die Boss dreht bschtendich um die griene Hiwwel un Baerrick rum darich die Schtaat Nei Yarick. Glei nochdem das sie in Pennsilfaani kumme, faahre sie newich em Susquehanna Rewwer her, wo er darich die Alleghenies schluppt. Wiewohl alsemol gleene Heemede sin unner an der Hiwwel, hot es net viel Bauerland eb sie noch Lengeschder Kaundi kumme.

Am Lengeschder Boss Depot kummt en Mann mit en breetranfdiche Hut aus en Maschien (wie die Schteetser en Kar heese), un griesst der Daed un der Levi mit Hand un Kuss. Weil es zu weit is fer in die Schtadt faahre mit Gaul un Karitsch, hot er en Mann mit en Maschien gedingt fer die Kanadaer abhole. Sie faahre der schmaale, grumme Weg nooch, zwische Bauereie mit grosse Heiser un annere Gebeier—alles weiss aagschtriche.

sylvania if Anna looks after the house, and if neighbor Paul drops in occasionally to see whether Menno needs help.

"There really isn't much that needs to be done right now," Father admits. "You may haul some manure on the corn land, and the children can help pick stones on Saturday. Watch out for bloating cows in this fresh pasture. If there is any trouble, get Paul to look at them. He can tell you whether to call the vet."

"Don't worry," Menno says. "We'll be all right."

Menno's parents have not traveled much since they were married, so they marvel at the sights they see: the Burlington Skyway, Lake Ontario, and the Welland Canal. They have just a glimpse of Niagara Falls, but it is a thrill just to know that they are so close. At Buffalo they cross the border and have their first look at the United States.

Through New York State, their public bus winds between green slopes. Soon after crossing into Pennsylvania, they follow the Susquehanna River as it snakes its way through the Alleghenies. Although there are occasional small homes at the foot of the slopes, there is hardly any farmland before they reach Lancaster County.

At the Lancaster bus depot, a man wearing a broad-brimmed hat steps from a waiting taxi and greets Father and Levi with a handshake and kiss. Because it is too far to drive to the city with the carriage, he has hired a taxi to meet the Canadians. They wind along narrow paved roads, between farms with large houses and other buildings, all painted white. When they arrive at their destination, women greet the visiting women with a kiss, and the men and women shake hands.

A large supper awaits the travelers. They begin the meal with a silent grace, just like the Canadian Mennonite custom, but after supper, they again give thanks to God. The men sit and visit while the women wash the dishes. Then the visitors walk across the road to the neighbors, where they spend the night and have breakfast.

Wann sie an die Heemet kumme, griesse die Weibsleit ennanner graad wie die Mannsleit hen, un die Mannsleit un Weibsleit gewwe ennanner "Wie gehts?"

En gross Nachtesse is em waarde fer die Reesende. Sie fange es Esse aa wie die Kanadaer daheem gegwehnt sin, mit en schtill Gebet, un noch em Esse danke sie widder. Die Mannsleit sitze (nee, hocke!) un bsuche, un die Weibsleit wesche es Gschaer, dann laafe sie all iwwer der Weg zu der Nochbere wo sie bleiwe iwwer Nacht un fer es Mariye-Esse.

An der acht Uhr der naegscht Mariye kumme die Nochbere vun iwwer em Weg mit ihrem Gaul un Karitsch fer helfe Kanadaer faahre. Die eent Paar faahrt mit der Leit wo sie's Nachtesse grickt hen, un die anner Paar mit die wo sie waare iwwer Nacht. Noch em Middaag handle sie rum. Sie mache drei Kaals Vammiddaags, un vier Nochmiddaags, so das sie zehe Bletz dreffe der Daag, mit der Esse-bletz.

Sunndaag Mariyets kumme sie frieh ans Wewerland Gmeehaus. Es sin lange Roihe Schepp ausser um der Hof rum, wo die Mannsleit schtehn un griesse Freind: Bekannde un Fremme. Es Watt is rumkumme das Kanadaer in der Gegend sin, so sie waerre bewillkummt vun viele. Die gheierde Mannsleit griesse sie all mit Hand un Kuss.

Der Daed guckt rum an die Fuhrwaericke. Er weest das die Lengeschder Leit als ken Gammreefe odder rubber tires ghat hen, un das die Yunge als top Boggis gfaahre hen. Yetzt hen sie ball all rubber tires. Es hot gaar ken uffniche Boggis odder Karitsches, un aa ken top Buggis. Yung un alt faahre yetzt Karitches wo ringsrum zu sin. Die Yunge ihre hen een Sitz; die Alde zwee.

In em Gmeehaus henke der Daed un der Levi ihre Hiet in es Schtiwwli un gehn nei in es gross Deel. Sie hocke newich eens vun der Fuhrmenner, naegscht vanne. Der anner Fuhrmann geht vaerri un hockt an der Singdisch in der Mitt, vannich em Breddichesdisch, wo die Vorsinger hocke. Der Daed verschtaunt sich wann eens vun der Vorsinger en Lied ausgebt un

At eight o'clock the following morning, their hosts of the evening before arrive with horse and carriage to help with transporting the Canadians and accompanying them from place to place during the day. One couple rides with their supper hosts, and the other rides with their overnight hosts. After dinner, they switch around. The group stays together all day, and different homes serve them the three meals. They make three other calls in the forenoon, and four more in the afternoon, making a total of ten stops for the day.

On Sunday, they arrive early at the Weaverland meeting-house. There are long rows of sheds around the sides of the yard, as shelter for the horses. Here the men stand to be greeted by friends, familiar ones and new ones. Word has spread that Canadians are in the community, so they are welcomed by many. All the married men, being church members, greet them with a kiss.

Father looks around at the vehicles. He had heard that steel tires were the norm, but he soon sees that most have rubber tires now. There are no open buggies or carriages. The married people have closed carriages, like covered buggies except that they are slightly longer and have two seats. The front seat folds forward to let the women get to the back seat. The young people traditionally rode in buggies with one seat and folding tops, but now most of them have closed one-seaters that they call carriages.

Inside the meetinghouse, Father and Levi hang their hats in the cloakroom, then follow the other men into the main room. They sit beside one of the drivers, near the front, while the other driver goes forward to sit at the singers' table, centered in front of the minister's bench and table. Father is surprised when one of the song leaders at the singers' table announces a hymn and starts singing before the ministers enter and sit on their bench.

There is no pulpit. Instead, a speaking preacher stands behind a small table. The congregation sings another hymn after

fangt aa singe, eb die Diener reikumme fer ihre Bletz nemme. Es hot ken Breddichschtul; yuscht en glee Dischli wo der Breddicher schteht fer reede. Noch en Lied waet gsunge nochdem das die Diener neikumme. Die Lieder sin bekannt, awwer der Daed kummt ball net mit der Weiss, weil es so viel uff un ab geht.

Es menscht vun der Versammling scheint bekannt. Der Eldeschde leest der Text ab noch der Vorreed, in Blatz vun vorher, un die Leit schtehn fer der Sege schpreche noch dem letschde Gebet. Es hot wennich Unnerschied in der Breddich, meh wie das ken zwee Breddicher sich gleich ausschpreche.

Der Unnerschied in der Gmee scheint net so marickwaddich zum Daed. Es is en greessere Unnerschied im daegliche Lewe. Die Lengeschder Mennischde hen ken rubber tires uff ihre Traekders. Sie hen Bang en Traekder fiehrt zu die Maschiene faahre uff em Weg. Der Daed verschteht selle Gfaahr vun sei Erfaahring daheem.

Wann sie aa Schtaalreef Traekders hen, sin die Lengeschder Leit doch meh neimodisch eigricht wie ihre Kossens in Kanada. Sie hen Stable Cleaners, Silo Unloaders, un Mechanical Feeders. Sie hen schunn lang Telefohns in der Heemede, wo die Woolwich Mennischde net ghat hen eb kaetzlich. Der Daed glaabt es is ball ewe verdeelt. Am End is es unmieglich fer saage well as recht odder letz is. Es Haupt is fer sich so viel wie mieglich abgsondert halde vun der Welt. Yeder Gegend muss sei eegne Addning hawwe fer des ausfiehre.

Die Yaahre gehn rum. Der Menno geht nau schunn unnerschiedliche Yaahre an die Singings. Alsemol geht er heem graad noch em Singes. Anneremol helft er schpiele. Dann un wann, demnooch mit wem das er is, geht er aa in es Weschhaus un helft danze. Die letscht Weil baddert sell ihn. Er weest das sei Eldre sell ungern hedde wann sie es wissde. Er fiehlt in der Schuld, net yuscht wehe em Danzes, awwer aa wehe anner

the ministers enter. The hymns are familiar, yet Father finds it difficult to follow the tune, with its extra slurs and twists.

Most of the service seems familiar. However, the deacon reads the selected Scripture text after the opening sermon instead of before it. In addition, after the last prayer, the congregation stands for the benediction. There is little difference in the style and content of the preaching, except for the obvious fact that no two ministers have the same way of expressing themselves.

The differences in the meeting do not seem important to Father. There are greater differences in everyday life. The Lancaster Mennonites have no rubber tires on their tractors. They fear that a tractor on rubber would soon be used for general transportation on the road, substituting for a car or truck. Father realizes this danger from experience at home.

In spite of their steel-wheeled tractors, the Lancastrians have more modern equipment than their Canadian cousins. They have stable cleaners, silo unloaders, and mechanical feeders. The Lancaster Mennonites have had phones in their homes for a long time; the Woolwich Mennonites did not have them until recently.

Father feels that these practices balance out rather evenly. After all, it is impossible to tell exactly which is right or wrong. The main idea is to keep separated from the world as much as possible and maintain close ties in the brotherhood. Each community must find its own method for accomplishing this.

The years roll by. Menno has been going to the singings regularly now for several years. Sometimes he goes home soon after they finish singing. Other times he joins in playing games. Sometimes, depending on what company he is in, he goes out to the washhouse and takes part in the square dancing.

Lately, the dancing has been bothering him. He knows that his parents would object if they knew. He feels guilty about the

Sach. Der meh das er driwwerdenkt, der meh kummt ihm in der Sinn wo er es verschult hot.

Noch eens kummt ihm in der Sinn. Er is yetzt achtzeh, ball neinzeh. Sell is die Elt wo viel Buwe sich daafe losse, wiewohl en Deel noch en Yaahr waarde. Die Maed gehn gwehnlich en Yaahr odder zwee yinger. Ferwas losst er sich net daafe un geht zu der Gmee? Bis des Zeit daed er gern es alt Lewe uffgewwe, fer es Gfiehl vun Schuld los waerre.

Um der erscht Moi macht der Bischof die Eilaading fer die wo die Daaf erlange welle. Der Menno schwetzt mit eens vun der Diener, un is eens vun der Erschde fer der Naame eigewwe. En Woch odder zwee schpeeder waerre die Neeme abgleese vun achtzich Deifling. Der Daag vun der erscht Unnerricht waet ausgsaat.

Die Deifling vun der ganze Umgegend, vun der dreizeh Versammling-Heiser, sin all gezaehlt fer in der gwehnlicher Versammling sei mariyets, wo Unnericht sei soll Nochmiddaags. Die Unnerricht waet ghalde an vier unnerschiedliche Versammling-Heiser, an der drei Uhr, schtarick Zeit, uff sex Sunndaage nochennanner.

Wann die Zeit kummt, nemmt der Menno sein Blatz mit der

dancing and many other things. The more he thinks over his life, the more acts of his disobedience he remembers. Another realization comes with these thoughts. He now is eighteen, almost nineteen. Many of the boys are baptized at this age, though some wait another year. Girls are frequently baptized a year or two younger than the boys. He asks himself, "Why not be baptized and join the church?" At this time, he feels that he would gladly give up the old life, if he could get rid of the guilty feeling.

Around the first of May, the bishop extends an invitation to those who desire to be baptized. Menno speaks privately to one of the ministers and is one of the first volunteers. A week or two later, after church a minister publicly reads the names of about eighty applicants from a cluster of congregations. The bishop announces the date for the first instruction meeting.

All the applicants from the thirteen meetinghouses are expected to attend Sunday morning services at the same place the afternoon instruction meeting is to be held for their particular area. For six successive Sundays, these meetings are held simultaneously at four or more meetinghouses, at three o'clock daylight saving time.

When the instruction time comes, Menno takes his place with the other applicants on the front benches in the meetinghouse. The boys sit on the elderly men's benches, and the girls sit facing them on the women's side. Around them, the house is filled to capacity. Although these services are especially for youth, they are open to all. About half as many adults attend as at regular services.

The meeting begins as usual except that the hymns for the occasion are songs for young people. The first is number 52, "Stop, Poor Child; Where Do You Haste?" This is the first in a sequence of twelve hymns sung at the afternoon services during the next six weeks.

After the hymn, a deacon reads a chapter from the New Testament: in this case, Hebrews 11, the faith chapter. Following

annere Deifling uff der vedderschde Daadi-Benk, un die Maed
uff der Mammi-Benk, gehenanner gedreht. Es Haus is ganz
voll. Wie wohl die Nochmiddaag Versammling es menscht is
fer die Yunge, sie is fer yederepper. Ungfaehr halwe so viel eldere Leit sinn datt wie an en gwehnliche Versammling.

Die Versammling fangt aa wie gwehnlich, awwer die Lieder
sin fer yunge Leit. Es erscht Lied is "Halt, armes Kind, wo
eilscht du hin?" Sell is es erscht Lied vun der zwelf wo gsunge
waerre die naegschde sex Sunndaag-Nochmiddaag.

Noch em Singes leest en Eldeschde en Kabiddel aus em Neie
Teschdament, desemol es elft Ebraer, es Kabbidel vum Glaawe.
Noch sellem reed eens vun der Breddicher vun em Text, dann
waet gegniet fer en schtilles Gebet. Noch sellem leest en annere
Breddicher der erscht Addickel (Dordrecht Glaawes Bekenntniss, 1632) wehe Gott un der Erschaffing alle Dinge. Er legt
der Addickel aus, leest noch en Paar annere Schriftschtelle, not
frogt er die Lehryinger eb sie es verschtehn un glaawe, dann
solle sie ihre Yawatt gewe, eens noch em annere.

Der dritt Breddicher leest nau der zwett Addickel ab, wehe
des Menschen Fall, noch der nehmliche Addning, un frogt fer
ihre Yawatt. Dann leest er noch der dritt Addickel ab, wehe
dem widder Uffrichdes vum Mensch darich Grischdes' Verschpreche. Wann die drei Addickel uffgnumme sin, un die
Yawadde gewwe dazu, schprecht er der Sege iwwer ihre Verschpreche, un frogt fer Zeignis vun der annere Diener. Die Versammling waett zum Schluss gebrocht im gwehnliche Weg, un
die Zeit un der Blatz fer die naegscht Nochmiddaag-Versamm-
ling waet ausgsaat.

Der Menno guckt vaerre zu der Unnerricht-Versammlinge
die naegschde sex Woche. Uff yeden Sunndaag waerre die
Lieder der Roi nooch gsunge, un en schicklich Kabiddel waet
abglese. Der zwett Sunndaag waerre der viert, finft, un sext
Addickel uffgnumme wehe Grischde Zukunft, es Effangelium
odder Nei Teschdament, un Buuss un Bessering des Lewes.

Der siwwet Addickel is wehe daafe. Als eens vun der Dei-

this, one of the preachers expounds on the text, then all kneel in silent prayer.

Next a second preacher reads the first of the eighteen "Articles of Faith" (Dordrecht, 1632), this one about God and the creation. He explains the meaning of the article, reads related Scripture verses, and otherwise instructs the students. When he finishes, he asks whether they understand and believe the content of the article. Each one replies in the affirmative.

The third preacher now reads the second article, on the fall of humanity, following the same procedure, and asking for their "Yeas." Then he reads the third article, on the restoration of humanity, through the promise of Christ's coming. When they have dealt with all three articles and affirmed them, the preacher invokes a blessing on the promises made and asks for testimony from the other ministers. The services are closed in the usual way, and the time and place for the next meeting is announced.

Menno looks forward to the meetings during the next six weeks. On each Sunday, they sing the hymns in their order, and a minister reads an appropriate chapter of Scripture. On the second Sunday, they explore the fourth, fifth, and sixth articles, about the coming of Christ to earth, the gospel of the New Testament, and the need for repentance.

The seventh article concerns baptism. As an applicant, Menno confesses that he believes in baptism to follow a confession of faith, grief for sin, repentance from sin, and a spiritual new birth. The eighth declares the church as the communion of saints, and the ninth touches on the election and offices of preachers and other servants of the church.

The tenth is about holy communion as a remembrance of Christ's suffering and death, and a reminder to love one another. The eleventh deals with the foot washing of saints, as instituted by Christ at the Last Supper. The twelfth is on matrimony as appointed by Christ. The thirteenth is about the governing authorities, teaching us to respect and obey the rulers

fling, bekennt der Menno das er glaabt an die Daaf uff Bekenntniss des Glaawes, Rei un Leed vun seine Sinde, un geischtlich widder gebore sei. Der Acht is vun der Gmeeschaft der Heiliche. Der Neint is wehe dem Diener aasetze.

Es Zehet is wehe em Nachtmohl, als en Gedechtnis vun Grischde Leides un Schtaerwes, un vun der Liewe unnichenanner. Des Elft is wehe em Fiesswesche, wie Grischdus es eigsetzt hot bei dem Nachtmohl. Es Zwelft handelt wehe heiere, wie Grischdus es eigsetzt hot. Es Dreizeht is vun em Amt der weltliche Owwerichkeit. Es Vaetzeht is gege der Rache, odder sich wehre. Grischdus hot aabefohle fer der anne Backe zu drehe, un unsere Feind liewe. Es Fuffzeht is gege Schweere. Es Sechzeht is wehe dem Bann odder Zrickschtelle. Es Siwwezeht is vun der Meiding vun denne wo zrickgschtellt sin. Es Achtzeht is vun dem widder Uffrichdes vun der Dode, un es letzt Gericht.

Uff der letscht Daag vun der Unnerricht, noch der gwehnliche Versammling, halde die Diener en Umfrog, wo dann die Gmeesglieder gfrogt waerre fer enniche Glaag, odder Ursach bringe das enniche vun der Deifling net aagnumme waerre kennde fer die Daaf erlange. Wann ken Glaag kummt, odder die Sach recht gmacht is, waert dann aagschtalt gmacht fer sie rischde zum Daafes.

Wann die Unnerricht verbei is, un die Glaawesaddickel aagnumme, dien die Diener die Zeit un Bletz ausgewwe fer daafe uff die naegschde zwee Sunndaage. (Die Daafiewing waet nau ghalde an sex Versammlingheiser.) Der Menno is eens vun denne wo gedaaft waerre uff der erscht Sunndaag. Samschdaag-Nochmiddaags vorher, sin sie beinanner am Versammlinghaus mit der Dienerschaft. Annere Gmeesglieder sin net gwehnlich dabei. Die Breddicher gehn nochemol iwwer die Glaawesaddickel, gewwe der Deifling Rot, un vermaahne sie zum grischdliche Glaawe, Liewe, un Geduld.

Wann der Menno an die Versammling kummt der naegscht Mariye, is der Hof schunn ganz voll. Em Menno sein Hals

insofar as they do not contradict the Christian faith.

The fourteenth concerns revenge, resistance, or the taking up of arms. Christ forbade carnal warfare, teaching his followers to turn the other cheek, and rather to suffer persecution than defend themselves or their property.

The fifteenth article is against the taking of oaths. Christ said, "Swear not at all. . . . Let your communication be yea, yea; nay, nay." The sixteenth is about excommunication of offenders. The seventeenth refers to avoidance of backsliders. The eighteenth speaks of the resurrection of the dead and the last judgment.

On the last day of the instruction meetings, following the regular morning service, the ministers hold an inquiry, asking church members to bring any complaints or reasons why any of the applicants should not be accepted for membership. If there are no complaints or if the faults are corrected, the ministers take further steps to prepare them for baptism.

When the instruction meetings are ended and all the articles of faith accepted, the ministers announce the dates of baptism for the following Sundays. Menno is one of a group of twenty who are baptized on the first Sunday. On the preceding Saturday afternoon, the group of twenty gathers at the meetinghouse with the ministry. Lay members do not usually attend. The ministers review the articles of faith, counsel the applicants, and exhort them to live in Christian faith, charity, and forbearance.

When Menno arrives at the meetinghouse the next morning, the yard is already quite crowded. A lump forms in Menno's throat when he thinks of the reason for the crowd. With the other applicants, he takes his place on the front bench, and the service begins in the usual manner. The text is John 1:1-36. The first preacher comments on the text.

After silent prayer, the bishop further exhorts the applicants. Then he stands in front of the pulpit, with the class in a semicircle around him. He asks them three questions:

waerd eng wann er draadenkt worum die Mensche do sin. Mit der annere Deifling nemmt er sein Sitz uff der vedderscht Bank; un die Versammling fangt aa wie gwehnlich. Der Text is Yohannes, 1:1-36. Der erscht Breddicher nemmt der Text uff. Noch em schtille Gebet, gebt der Bischof noch weidere Vermaahning. Dann schtellt er sich vannich der Breddichschtul, mit die Deifling ausser um ihn rum. Er schtellt die drei Froge:

Eb sie glaawe an Gott, der Himmel un Erd erschaffe hot; an Yeesus Grischdus, der Sohn Gottes, als eier Erleeser, un an der Heilich Geischt, der ausgeht vum Vadder un dem Sohn? Hoscht du dei Sinde bereiet, un dein eegener Wille un die Werke des Satans verlosse? Verschprechscht du, darich Gottes Gnade un Beischtand, die Lehre Yeesu Grischde zu folge bis in den Dod?

Wann die Deifling ihre Yawatt gewwe hen zu der drei Froge, gniet der Bischof mit der Deifling nunner, un die Iwweriche Versammelde schtehn uff; dann fiehrt der Bischof en laut Gebet. Am End schteht der Bischof uff, die Deifling bleiwe gegniet, un die Iwweriche sitze anne. Een Eldischde kummt vaerri mit en Kiwweli mit Wasser, un en Koppli, un schteht uff em Bischof sei rechtse Seit. Der Bischof legt sei Hend uff em erschde Deifling sein bludde Kopp, un schprecht die Wadde aus:

Auf des Bekenntniss deines Glaubens, Reu und Leid deiner Sinden, wirscht du getauft [*dann formt er en Koppli mit sei Hend, wo der Eldeschde en wennich Wasser neileert*] mit Wasser, im Namen des Vaters, und des Sohnes, und des Heiligen Geischtes.

So gehn sie der Roi nooch.

Unner dereweil nemmt em Eldeschde sei Fraa die Kapp vun yedes vun der Maed ihre Kepp, un gebt sie dem Bischof sei Fraa, wo die Kappe uff der Maed ihre Kepp setzt noch dem das sie gedaaft sin. Wann sie all gedaaft sin, geht der Bischof

Do you believe in God, who created heaven and earth; in Jesus Christ, the Son of God, as your Savior; and in the Holy Spirit, flowing from the Father and Son? Have you repented from sin, and are you willing to forsake your own will and the works of Satan? Do you promise, through God's grace and guidance, to follow the teachings of Christ until death?

When the applicants have given their word of consent to all three questions, the bishop and applicants kneel, and the bishop offers vocal prayer. At the end of the prayer, the bishop rises, while the class remains kneeling (heads toward the front). A deacon steps forward with a pail of water and a cup. He stands at the right hand of the bishop, who places his hands on the bare head of the first applicant and pronounces the following words:

Upon the confession of your faith, repenting and grieving for your sins, you are baptized [*at this moment, the bishop forms a loose funnel with both hands, into which the deacon pours a small amount of water that runs onto the head*] with water, in the name of the Father, Son, and Holy Ghost.

In this way, they go from one to the next.

Meanwhile, the deacon's wife lifts the cap or prayer covering from each young woman's head in turn just before the baptism, and the bishop's wife replaces it after baptism. When all have been baptized, the bishop returns to the first one, grasps his right hand to raise him, and says,

In the name of the congregation, I offer you my hand; arise to a new beginning. May the Lord transfer you from your sinful condition into the righteousness of his kingdom. Be therefore welcomed as a brother in the congregation.

With that, he salutes the new brother with the kiss of peace. He follows the same procedure with the young women, except

zrick zu dem Erschde, nemmt sei rechtse Hand fer ihn uffschtelle, un saagt:

Im Namen der Gemeinde biete ich dir die Hand; richt du dich
auf zu einem neuen Anfang. Der Herr wolle dich versetzen
aus deinem Sindenstand in die Gerechtigkeit seines Reichs,
Sei jetzt willkomm als ein Bruder (Schwester) der Gemeinde.

Mit dem griesst er der nei Bruder mit dem Kuss des Friedens.
Er geht der nehmliche Addning nooch mit der Maed, yuscht er
griesst sie als Schweschter, un sei Fraa griesst sie mit dem Kuss.
Wann es Daafes ausgfiehrt is, nemme die Deifling ihre Sitz,
un der Bischof geht hinnich der Breddichschtul. Dann leest er
es sext Kabiddel an die Reemer, un verhandelt es noch en wennich. Dann folgt en Gebet, un die Versammling waet zum
Schluss gebrocht.

Der Menno is dief bewoge noch der Zeremonie. Er hot gaar
ken Verlange meh noch der weltliche Lischde un Blessiere.
Yuscht, oh, weh! Des is zu gut fer halde. Es geht net lang bis
der Versucher widder kummt fer ihn widder verfiehre. Der
Kamf halt aa fer es iwwerich vun seim Lewe. Mecht er doch
kemfe bis ans End!

Wann der Menno yetzt gedaaft is, hot er es Recht fer es
Nachtmohl nemme, un hot in allem die nehmlich Freiheit wie
annere Gmeesglieder. Er hett aa es Recht fer in der Rot geh an
der Umfrog, yuscht im Gebrauch gehn yuscht die eldschte
Glieder in der Rot.

Die Umfroge waerre zweemols Yaahr ghalde eb Nachtmohl.
Im Frieyaahr sin sie uff die letschde drei Sunndaage vor den
Oschdere. Im Schpotyaahr sin sie die letschde drei Sunndaage
vor der Ernversammling, wo Blatz nemmt Donnerschdaags eb
der erscht Freidaag im September. Uff em Umfrog Daag is der
Text es achtzeht Matteus. Die Breddich is gegrindt uff Liewe
un Langmut.

Noch dem das die gwehnlich Versammling aus is, bleibt der

that he welcomes them as sisters and his wife salutes them with a kiss.

With the baptism completed, the young people resume their seats, and the bishop again takes his place behind the pulpit. He reads the sixth chapter of Romans and discusses Christian life and obedience. The bishop follows with prayer and the customary ending.

Menno is deeply moved by this ceremony. Afterward, he has no desire whatever for worldly lusts and pleasures. But alas! this state is too good to remain. It is not long before the tempter is at hand to drag him down again. The battle goes on for the rest of his life. May the Man of Heaven win!

Now that Menno is baptized, he is entitled to partake of communion and all the other privileges enjoyed by members. He may also give counsel in the church meetings, though in practice only the older members do that.

Counsel meetings are held twice a year, before communion. In the spring, they are held on the last three or four Sundays before Easter. In the fall, they are on the last three Sundays before the harvest meeting, which falls on the Thursday before the first Friday in September. On the day of a counsel meeting, the text is Matthew 18. The sermon's theme is love and forbearance.

After the close of the regular service, Menno remains seated, along with the other church members. The ministers then retire to the small cloakroom, which doubles as a counsel chamber. The older members follow into the counsel room in groups, first the men and then the women. In turn, each member offers his hand to the ministers, confesses peace with God and fellow members, and expresses a desire to partake of communion.

If any member has a complaint or suggestion to make regarding the ordinances or their observance, he is at liberty to express himself. If a complaint is directed at a certain individual, the complainer is expected to have attempted a reconciliation beforehand (Matt. 18:15). Otherwise, the ministers do

Menno sitze mit der iwweriche Glieder. Die Diener gehn not naus in es Mammi-Schtiwweli, wo aa gezaehlt is fer es Rot-Kemmerli. Die eldschde Glieder gehn dann naus in der Rot in Gruppe, erscht die Mannsleit, not die Weibsleit. Eens noch em annere gewwe sie die Hand zu der Diener, bekenne der Friede mit Gott un Mensche, un eissere sich wehe ihrem Verlange fer mit zum Nachtmohl geh.

Wann sie enniche Glaag zu bringe hen, wehe wie die Addninge ausgfiehrt waerre, hen sie yetzt die Glegeheit fer sich ausschpreche. Wann sie awwer en Glaag hen gehe en Gmeesglied, is es gezaehlt das sie erscht gsucht hen sich zu versehne mit ihm eb sie en Glaag bringe (Matt. 18:15); wann net, waet's net abgnumme. Nochdem das die Gruppe all draus waare, kumme die Diener widder rei an ihre Bletz, un eens vun ihne bringt der Rot vor was neikumme is.

Zweemols Yaahr, uff em Freidaag noch Oschdre im Friehyaahr, un Freidaags noch Ernversammling im Schpotyaahr, is der Diener ihre Zammekunft. Datt waet der Umfrog-Rot verhandelt, un waet gebraucht fer die Gmee-Addning widder uffsetze fer es naegscht halb Yaahr. Die Gmee waet viel uff die nehmlich Aart gfiehrt wie unser Owwerichkeit; yuscht der Bischof is net aagsehne wie en hoche Amtsmann. Er is naecher wie en Vorsitzer. Die Regel un Addning waerre gmacht bei der Gmeesglieder, graad so viel wie bei dem Bischof.

Uff em Sunndaag nein Daag noch der Zammekunft fange die Nachtmohle aa, un halde aa fer finf Woche. Wann en Paar gleene Gegende zammegehn, kenne die drei Bischof sie so-zunot all bediene in finf Woche.

Es Nachtmohl waet alsemols es Liewesmahl odder es Gedechtnissmahl gheese. Die Mennischde glaawe net das Grischdus leibhafdich in em Brot un Wei is. Sie sehne es yuscht als en Figur. Fer es erscht is es en Figur vun em Passah Fescht. (2 Mose 12), wo die Israelite en Schippli gschlacht hen, un ihre Daereposchde un Schwelle aagschtriche hen mit dem Blut, so das der Engel verbei geht.

not accept the complaint. After all the groups of men and women have been to the counsel room, the ministers return to their places, and the bishop or the home preacher presents the counsel given by the members.

Twice a year, on the Friday following Easter in the spring, and the Friday following harvest meeting in the fall, the ministers hold their conference. They deal with issues of the counsel meetings and may use them as a basis for future church policy. In fact, the church is governed in much the same way as our democratic government. The bishops are not considered as high-ranking officials; they serve more in the capacity of moderators. The members themselves make the rules or laws.

On the Sunday nine days after the conference, communion services begin. Since three bishops administer communion to the congregations, they can only serve it at three places each Sunday, and it takes five weeks to get around. Several of the congregations go together, so there is communion at fifteen places instead of eighteen.

Communion is also known as the Lord's Supper, the love feast, or the remembrance feast. The Mennonites do not believe in transubstantiation, that Christ is bodily present in the eucharist. Instead, they consider the bread and wine of communion as symbols.

First, the bread and wine are symbolic of the Passover feast (Exod. 12). Then the Israelites were required to partake of a lamb without spot or blemish, and to paint the side posts and lintels of their doorways with the blood, as a sign for the angel of death to pass over.

Second, they are symbolic of the Lamb of God, who gave his body and shed his blood on the cross. This makes it possible for the angel of everlasting death to pass over those who accept Christ as their Lord and Savior.

On communion Sunday, the first hymn illustrates Christ's suffering and death. A deacon reads either Matthew 26 or Luke 22. The home preacher then delivers a sermon—not from the

Fer's zwett is es en Figur vum Lamm Gottes, wo sei Blut vergosse hot am Greitz, so das der Engel vum ewiche Dod an uns verbei geht, wo ihn aagnumme hen als unser Erleser un Seelichmacher.

Am Nachtmohl-Sunndaag is es erscht Lied en Figur vun Grischde Leides un Schterwes. En Eldeschde leest endwedders Matteus 26 odder Luke 22. Der Heemdiener bringt die Vorreed; net aus dem Text, awwer vun der Schepfung bis zu der Israelite im Lande Gosen. Die Hauptgwicht waet glegt uff Schticker wo anneweise zu Grischde Erscheining.

Noch dem Gebet leest der zwett Eldeschde es folgende Gabbidel ab: Matteus 27 odder Luke 23. Uff des verhandelt der Bischof vun der Israelite ihre Rees aus Egypte noch Canaan. Dann leest er noch die Selbscht-briefing Schrift, 1 Korinther 11:23-34, un geht dann in es Gebet.

Der Eldeschde nemmt not der Deller, mit Brot in Zoll-Schtraeme gschnidde, un schtellt es uff der Breddichschtul. Die Leit schtehn all uff, un der Bischof schprecht der Sege iwwer es Brot. Wann die Leit widder sitze, brecht er en Brocke Brot ab, un esst es selwer, dann gebt er yedem Glied en Brocke der Roi nooch. Dieweil der Bischof es Brot ausdeelt, dutt er schickliche Schrifde iwwerhole.

Wann es Brot ausgedeelt is, nemmt der Bischof widder sein Sitz. Der Eldeschde fillt en Koppli mit Wei, un schtellt es uff der Breddichschtul. Die Leit schtehn widder uff, un der Bischof schprecht der Sege iwwer der Wei. Wann sie widder all sitze, nemmt der Bischof selwer en Schluck, un gebt es Koppli zu yedem Glied der Roi nooch, das yedes en Schluck nemmt. Es waet en Lied gsunge dieweil der Wei ausgedeelt waet.

Die Versammling waet not zum End gebrocht mit Zeignis, Gebet, en Lied singe, un der Sege schpreche. Der Bischof leest noch Johannes 13:1-17, wo handelt vun Grischde Befehl wehe Fiess wesche. Not is die Hauptversammling aus, yuscht die Glieder waerre gfrogt fer noch sitze bleiwe.

Unner dereweil hen zwee Eldeschde Wasser grischt in

text, but from Genesis, beginning with the creation, and continuing up to the time of Israel's entry into the land of Goshen. He places special emphasis on those events that relate to Christ's coming.

After the prayer, a second deacon reads the following chapter, either Matthew 27 or Luke 23. After this, the bishop preaches on Moses, the Israelites' exodus, and their travels to Canaan. When he finishes, he reads 1 Corinthians 11:23-34, pointing the congregation to self-examination. Then he leads them in prayer.

The deacon takes a platter of bread, already cut into one-inch square strips, which he places on the pulpit. The congregation stands, and the bishop asks the blessing on the bread. When all are seated again, the bishop breaks off a portion of bread, partakes, and then metes out a morsel to each member, while the deacon follows with the plate. While passing out the bread, the bishop quotes numerous related Scriptures.

When all have partaken of the bread, the bishop resumes his seat. The deacon pours a cup of wine, which he places on the pulpit. Again, the congregation stands while the bishop asks the blessing on the wine. After all are seated again, the bishop takes a sip, then passes the common cup to all the members, who each take a sip in turn. While this is in progress, the people sing a hymn.

The service moves toward closing in the regular way with testimony, prayer, a hymn, and benediction. Then the bishop reads John 13:1-17 and comments on Christ's commandment to his followers to wash each other's feet. As the bishop closes the communion service, he gives children and other nonmembers a chance to leave but asks members to remain seated for the aftermeeting foot washing observance.

Meanwhile, two deacons have prepared water in wooden basins, placing some for the men before the front benches, with towels alongside; and likewise in the cloakrooms for the women. The members come forward, two by two, wash and

holziche Ziwwerlin. Die eent Helft schtelle sie vannich die
Mannsleitbenk, un die annere in es Schtiwweli fer die Weibsleit; mit Handdicher newedraa. Die Glieder kumme vaerre,
zwee bei zwee, wesche ennanner die Fiess, un butze sie ab;
dann gewwe sie ennanner der Kuss des Friedens. En schicklich
Lied waet gsunge dabei. Wann sie all faeddich sin, un hen ihre Sitz widder gnumme,
leest der Bischof der Zammekunft-Schluss ab. Es hot en Roi vun
Sache wo im Abschnitt sin, un noch en Roi wo dagehe gezeigt
sin. Die Glieder waerre vermaahnt fer gedrei sei, un fer der Zammekunft-Schluss reschpekte; not is die Versammling aus.

Es verschteht sich selwer das des alles Zeit nemmt; ebmols
schier vier Schtund. Die wo weit hen, kumme net heem viel vor
der drei Uhr.

dry each other's feet, and salute each other with the kiss of peace. A fitting hymn is sung during the ceremony.

When all have finished and resumed their seats, the bishop reads the resolutions and decisions of the conference. There is one list of prohibited items, and another of those that are advised against. The bishop admonishes the congregation to faithfulness and respect for the decisions of the conference, and dismisses the people.

The whole process takes a considerable length of time, as much as four hours. Those who have far to go may not reach home before three o'clock.

Uff sei Eeyes

WANN DER MENNO eenezwanzich is, denkt er vun en Bauerei fer sich selwer. Gude Bauereie sin raar un deier; un em Menno sein Daed is net reich. Sie denke dann vun sich zufridde mache mit en Bauerei wo yuscht en gleene, schlechde Scheier hot. Sell mehnt en neie Scheier baue.

Viel gude Scheiere naegscht bei der grosse Schtedt sin nimme gebraucht, drum dien die Mennischde oft so Scheiere nunneroppe, un es Bauholz heemnemme fer neie Scheiere baue mit. Als der erscht Schritt, gehn der Menno, sein Daed, un der Schreiner-Baass, mit en gedingde alde Bauer mit seim Kar fer en Scheier suche. Wann sie eene finne wo sie denke as hielenglich waer, laade sie dreissich odder vaetzich Mann un Buwe ei fer helfe sie nunnerreise.

Uff der Daag wo ausgmacht is fer geh, gehn en Bosslood Mann mit Hammer, Schlegel, Schtange, un Schtrick, uff der Weg noch der Scheier. Wann sie annekumme, gehn der Menno un ungfaehr zwansich annere yunge Menner uff es Dach, un fange aa es runnerroppe. Die iwweriche roppe die Wedderbord ab, un reise die Frucht-Kammer raus. Bis Middaag is alles hunne wie es Gschtell.

So gschwindt wie die Esse-Kiwwel leer sin, gehn sie widder draa. En Deel vun der Gschickde graddele nuff fer die Schparre runnernemme, die Zappe rausdreiwe, un Schtrick feschtmache. Dann losse sie die Perleins un Dachpedde runner mit Schtrick.

Not mache sie Schtrick owwer an es erscht Bent fescht: eene nauszus, un eene neizus. Die iwweriche Zappe was es Bent noch fescht binne, waerre rausgschlaagge, un so viel Mann wie mieglich an die Schtrick, fer es saachde runnerlosse in die

On His Own

WHEN MENNO is twenty-one, he starts thinking about a farm of his own. Good farms are scarce and expensive, and Menno's father is not rich, so they decide to buy him a farm with a small, dilapidated barn. This involves building a new barn.

Many good barns near the cities are no longer in use, so the Mennonites dismantle some of them and use the material for building new barns or additions. As the first step, Menno, his father, and a carpenter hire a retired farmer with a car to take them on a barn hunt. When they find one that they think will be suitable, they recruit thirty or forty men and boys to help in dismantling it.

On the appointed day, a busload of men, armed with hammers, crowbars, sledge hammers, and ropes, head for the barn. When they arrive, Menno and about twenty other young men climb on the roof and start tearing it off. The rest remove the granary and siding. By dinnertime, the barn has been stripped down to the frame. Then comes the hard work.

After emptying their lunch baskets, the men go back to work. Several of the most nimble climb to the top plates, fasten ropes, and drive out the pins holding the skeleton together. They lift the plate off the tenons, while the men below lower it with the ropes. Next, they lower the purlins in the same way.

Now the "high riggers" fasten ropes to the top of the first bent, with one end of each rope on the outside and the other on the inside. They drive out the pins, separating the bent from the rest of the frame. All available hands hang onto the outside rope, as the bent is lowered to the barn floor. In this way, all five bents are lowered.

Scheier. Schnell waet es ausnannergnumme, un die Bleck nausgedraage, un die iwweriche Bents graad so runnerglosst.

Em Menno sein Daed hot en grosse flatbed Semitrailer annebschtellt fer kumme an der halb Vier, dann fange sie aa ufflaade. Bis finf Uhr is alles uffglaade, un die Mann sin uff em Heemweg.

Dieweil der Menno un sein Daed, mit der Nochbere ihre Hilf, es Fundament mache, legt der Schreiner un sei Mann die Scheier aus. Es brauch en Deel neie Bleck, un en wennich Rumenneres, so en Deel vun der Bleck misse iwwergmacht waerre.

Die Schreiner brauche abaddich Werkzeich fer die Aerwet, so wie en Bohrmaschien, en runder Meesel, un en Dexel. Die Tscheensaeg waet yetzt gwehnlich aa gebraucht dabei. Der Schreiner merkt die Bleck all, wo yede Schtick anne soll. Wann alles recht an der Blatz basst, dann kennt die Scheier schteh unne Neggel. Es macht der Menno denke an em Solomon sein Tempel, wo alles zammegebasst hot unne das mer en Hammer odder Ax gheert hot. Net das en Scheier baue so ruhich hergeht wie sell!

Die Nochbere un Freind vun weit un breet kumme bei fer helfe die Scheier uffschtelle. Es sin iwwer en hunnert Leit in all, un ungfaehr dreissich Weibsleit fer Esse mache. Der Schreiner schlenkert sei Winkeleise un ruft bei allem Lebdaag, dieweil er die Leit hieweist fer die Bleck neidraage. Wann sie draa sin die naegschde Bleck neidraage, macht er der erscht Bent zamme, un schlaagt die Zappe nei.

"Kummet all her!" ruft er. "Kummet um der Bent rum!"

Die Mann schtehn in en Roi un nemme halt.

"Sin dir reddi? Yo hie! Yo hie!"

Es Bent kummt ab vum Bodde.

"Yo hie! Yo hie! Grieyet eier Schteiber nei! Yo hie!"

Wann die Schteiber am Blatz sin ungfaehr vier Fuuss vum Bodde, halde sie ei fer schnaufe.

"Yo hie! Grieyet eier Schpiess nei! Yo hie! Henket an die Schtrick! Yo hie!"

Menno's father has ordered a flatbed semitrailer to haul the timbers. It is scheduled to arrive at 3:30. As each bent is lowered, the men drive out the pins and load the timbers on the truck. From ten to twenty men can load a beam by hand. By five o'clock the barn is down, the timbers loaded, and the men homeward bound.

Menno and his father build the foundation walls with the help of neighbors. The carpenter and his crew work at framing the new barn. A few of the timbers need to be replaced, and they need to make some changes in the barn, so they have to reframe some of the timbers.

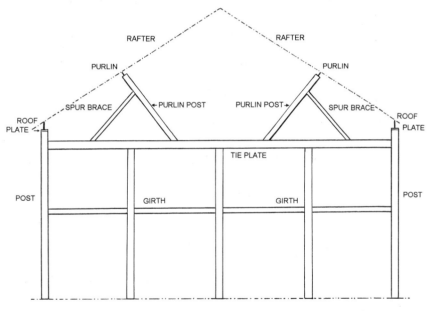

Bent Frehmes/Bent Framing

Schparre	rafter	*Schpannpett*	tie plate
Perlein	purlin	*Poschde*	post
Schporebuk	spur brace	*Gaett*	girth
Dachpett	roof plate		

Wann es Bent uffrecht schteht, binne sie es mit Schtrick, un schtelle es naegscht Bent uff, der nehmlich Weg. Die zwee Bent waerre zammegebunne mit Gaette. Des halt aa bis es ganz Gschtell uffrecht schteht bis Middaag.

Die Mannsleit wesche sich in Weschziwwer eb sie sich annesetze zu en lange Disch im Hof. Die Maed sin bissi am Gschaerre uff-fille. Es hot genunk Blatz fer abaud die Helft vun der Mann uff ee Zeit am esse sei. Der Menno is woll hungerich, awwer er waart bis es zwettmol rum.

Noch em Middaag waerre erscht die Schparre nuffgeduh, not die Schieting un Blech. Die eldere Mann sin am Wedderbord draanaggele. Bis Owed is die Scheier alles zu. Der Menno is mied un doch froh. Yetzt steht en Scheier wo geschder kenne war.

In em Yaahr noch seim Daafes, gehn em Menno sei Gedanke oft zurick an die Unnerricht. Er denkt oft an die liebliche Vermaahninge vum Bischof un der Breddicher. Er denkt an die

The carpenters need special tools for framing. They use a power wood drill and a chisel for cutting out the mortises and an adze for squaring timbers. The chain saw is now generally replacing older methods, especially for cutting and shaping the tenons. The carpenter has marked all the timbers before dismantling, so he knows where each piece goes. When all the framing is properly done and all the pins are in place, the frame would stand without nails.

Menno remembers Solomon's temple, which was fitted together so that no sound of hammer or axe was heard on-site while the men were building it. A barn raising is not such a quiet affair, though!

All the neighbors and friends from near and far gather for the raising. In all, there are over a hundred men. Around thirty women prepare dinner. The carpenter swings his square and shouts above the hubbub, directing the men to carry the proper timbers to the barn floor. While the men carry in the timbers, he assembles the first bent and drives home the pegs.

"All together!" he shouts. "Gather around the bent."

The men line up, taking hold of the tieplate.

"Ready? Yo heave! Yo heave!"

The bent starts to move.

"Yo heave! Get your shores in! Yo heave!"

With the shores or props in place, about four feet from the floor, the men pause for a breather.

"Yo heave! Get your pike poles! Yo heave! Heavy on the ropes! Yo heave!"

When the bent stands straight, it is tied in place with ropes. The next bent is raised in the same way. The two bents are tied together with girths. This continues until the whole frame is standing in place by dinnertime (noon).

The men wash up in washtubs before they sit down to the long row of tables on the lawn. The girls keep filling the dishes. There is room for about half of the men to eat at once. Menno is quite hungry but waits to eat with the second round.

Ehrfurcht un Gebeigtheit was er sell Zeit gschpiert hot. Er denkt an die Freindlichkeit was er gschpiert hot gehe die iwweriche Deifling. Dazu kummt ihm als widder in Sinn vun eem Gsicht was oft vor ihm war darich die Unnericht.

Der Menno kennt net saage was es is das ihn zu ihre ziegt. Sie guckt net schenner wie viel vun der annere Maed. Sie waert ken brechdiche Gleeder, wie wohl ihre Gleeder net es aller eefachscht waare. Deel Zeide hot sie abgharicht mit gnauer Uffmerksamkeit. Annere Zeide hot sie geguckt wie wann sie zu deemiedich un verzaagt waer fer uffgucke. *Ernschthaft* odder *sittsam* waer vielleicht der bescht Weg fer es auslege.

Mit en wennich Rumschpiones findt der Menno noch mehner aus wehe der Grace Weber. Ihren Daed is ken Bauer. Sie wohne in Yakobschteddel, wo er Karpets webt, un hot en gleener Schtor. Die Grace helft im Schtor wann sie net im Daaglohn schafft. Sie is en Yaahr yinger wie der Menno.

Wann der Menno aryetz in en annere Mennischde odder Amische Gegend wohne daed, not daed er waahrscheinlich sie yetzt froge fer en "Deet" fer en paar Mol, fer sie besser bekannt waerre. So wie es is, frogt er net fer sie sehne bis er in Ernscht is. Wann er ihre en Brief schreibt, un frogt fer sie heemfaahre vun Singing, un sie verschprecht, is es verschtanne das sie yetzt minanner gehn. Sie laenne das sich selwet uffgewwe en weider Weg geht um enanner zu verschteh un verdraage.

Es erscht Mol das der Menno sie heemnemmt, laad er sie ab an der vetterscht Daer, un geht heem. Er nemmt sie net in die Aerm un busst sie, weil sie ausgmacht hen fer die Hend ablosse vun ananner. Viel yunge Paar gehn alsnoch ins Bett minanner (mit der Gleeder aa) wie der alt Gebrauch waar. In der letschde Yaahre sin als meh wo sich halde das sie net naecher zammekumme wie newichnanner sitze im Boggi.

Wann der Menno die Grace eemol bsucht in ihre Heemet, weisst sie ihn darich es Haus. In viel Weg findt er es annerscht wie in sei Heemet. Sie hen Heidroh in der Heemet, un der Fohn in em Schtor. Sie hen hees un kalt Wasser in der Kich un

After dinner, the rafters are put up first, then the sheathing and the steel roofing. The older men are putting on siding. By evening, the barn is all closed in. Menno is tired but happy. His barn now stands where none stood yesterday.

During the year following his baptism, Menno's thoughts often turn back to the instruction meetings. He thinks of the loving admonition of the bishop and the preachers. Menno remembers the feeling of reverence and humility he experienced at that time. He recalls the kinship he felt with the rest of the class. Above all, a picture haunts his mind. He remembers one particular person whom he often faced on the opposite bench.

Menno can't make up his mind what she has that attracts him. She is no prettier than many other girls. She does not dress in flashy clothes, although her clothes are not the plainest. At times, she looked toward the instructor with rapt attention. At other times, she looked meek and humble, hardly daring to look up as she listened. Perhaps *demure* would best describe her.

By casual inquiries, Menno learns more about Grace Weber. Her father is not a farmer. They live in St. Jacobs, where he weaves rugs and operates a small store. Grace helps in the store when she is not working out by the day. She is a year younger than Menno.

If Menno lived in some other Mennonite or Amish community, he would probably date Grace several times to become better acquainted. As it is, he will not date her until his mind settles on his positive intentions toward her. Eventually he writes her a letter, asking permission to take her home from singing. If she consents, it is understood that they are now going together.

The first time Menno takes her home, he drops her off at the front door and goes home. They do not hug or kiss, as they have decided on hands-off courtship. Many young couples still

der Baadschtubb. Es sin weisse Dicher an der Fenschdere, an Blatz vun griene Fenschterdicher.

Eens vun der Schtuwwe uff em Schpeicher is der Grace ihre sauwere Schtubb. Es Hausrot Sach is alles der Grace ihres. Ihre Bett is zugedeckt mit eens vun ihre neie Gwilts. Es Seidbord, der Dresser, un der Byuuroo waare net nei, awwer sie hot sie selwer zweeg-gmacht. Owwer uff der Schenk sin die Gschenke wo sie grickt hot iwwer em Fattschaffe; schee Gschaer, gschaerrich un glaasich.

Die Grace macht die Daerlin vun der Schenk uff, un weisst em Menno ihre Gwilts un Maetts. Sie saagt ihm das sie ihre eegene Maetts heegelt, un schtickelt ihre eegene Gwilts. Ihre Maetts sin vun frische Farewe, mit Blumme un Veggel druff. Es menscht vun der Lumbe fer die Maetts heegle, kumme vun aldi Gleeder, awwer sie yuust noch en wennich Fils dazu, fer es mehner farwich mache.

Sie hot unnerschiedliche faeddiche Gwilts, un eene das sie am schtickle is, ball reddi fer gwilde. Weil em Menno sei Schweschdere noch yinger sin, un hen noch net viel Zeit ghat fer schaffe an Gwilts un Maetts, saagt die Grace ihm en wennich wehe ihre Gwiltaerwet.

"Mei faeddiche Gwilts sin en Blockhaus, en Peineppel, un en Weg im Sand. Der was ich gschtickelt hab, reddi fer gwilde, is en Mariye-Schtaenn. Wie viel Schticker denkscht du das in sellem Gwilt sin?"

"Oh, baut drei hunnert?"

"Ich hab es selwer ball net glaawe kenne bis ich sie gezaehlt hab. Es sin graad ee dausend Schticker. Yeder Blacke hot vaetzich Schticker, un es sin finfezwansich Blacke."

"Naehscht du all selle Schticker zamme bei Hand?"

"Oh nee!" lacht die Grace. "Ich hett net der Geduld fer sell. Es Gwildes waet vun Hand geduh, awwer ich duh es Schtickles uff der Naehmaschien."

"Wie schneitscht du all die gleene Schticker? Legscht du es Schtofft zamme, un schneitscht baut vier uff en Mol?"

go to bed for courting, fully dressed, according to the old custom called bundling. In recent years, an increasing number are adopting a form of courtship that does not involve closer contact than sitting together in the buggy.

When Menno visits Grace at her home a few weeks later, she shows him through the house. He finds many ways in which it differs from his home. They have hydroelectric power in their home and a phone in the store. There is hot and cold water on tap in the kitchen and bathroom. The windows have curtains instead of blinds.

Across the upstairs hall from her own bedroom, Grace shows Menno the spare bedroom where she keeps her own furniture. The bed is covered with one of her new quilts. She purchased the sideboard, dresser, and chest of drawers secondhand, and refinished them herself. While working as a hired girl, she received gift items, fine china and glassware, that adorn the tops of the furniture. Menno admires her keepsakes and realizes she has a start toward furnishing her own home.

Grace opens the dresser and sideboard doors to show Menno her quilts and hooked rugs. She tells him that she hooks all her own rugs and pieces her own quilts. Her rugs are brightly-colored, patterned with birds and flowers, but no scenery. Most of the material for hooking comes from used clothing, but she uses some bright felt to add variety.

She has several finished quilts and one quilt top that she is piecing; it is almost ready for quilting. Menno's sisters are younger and have little time for hooking rugs or quilting, so Grace tells him about her work on the quilts.

"My finished quilts are a Log Cabin, a Pineapple, and a Footprints in the Sand. I have pieced this Morning Star quilt top, and it is ready for us to sew it together. How many pieces do you think there will be in the quilt?"

"Oh, about three hundred?"

"There are exactly one thousand pieces. I could hardly believe it myself until I counted them. Each block has forty

"Verleicht daed ich, wann ich nei Schtofft kaafe daed davor. Guck mol: mir kaafe ken nei Schtofft fer es menscht vun unsere Gwilts, as wie fer der Granz un die Leining. Es menscht schneit ich aus Iwwerbleibsel vun Gleeder mache. En Deel vun em Hellgeduhn is noch iwwerich vun meiner Bobbi-Gleeder.

"Guck, es brauch yuscht drei Muschdere fer en Mariye Schtaenn mache: die gleene Eckschtee, die greessere Dreiecke, un die grosse Vierecke. Ich hab drei bappedeckliche Muschdere wo ich uff es Duch leg, un schneid drum rum. Ich kann Eckschtee aus zimmlich gleene Schticker schneide."

"Waer's net leichter fer en gross Schtick Schtofft kaafe, un es zammenaehe fer en Gwilt?"

"Un all die gleene Schticker Schtofft verhause? Un sell is net all," der Grace ihre Aage glitzere, "guck emol all der Gschpass was mir verfehle deede."

"Un wo daedscht all die Gschwetze ausfinne wann's ken Gwildings het?" zaerft der Menno.

"Ich misst mich uff dich verlosse fer's ausfinne iwwer em Scheiere baue," antwatt die Grace. "Ich hoff ich kann die Blacke folschder zammenaehe mariye, un am Dinschdaag der Gwilt in es Freem duh. Mir hen geplaennt fer Gwilding mache am Mittwoch."

Wann der Menno sehne kennt was alles am geh is Dinschdaags, daed er sich noch mehner verschtaune wehe em Gwildes. Die Grace un ihre Maem schpelle die Leining in es Freem, die nehmlich Grees wie der Gwilt. Not lege sie der flaumich Gwilt-Baett druff, un der gschtickelt Gwilt datt owwer druff, un schpelle alles zamme. Dann merkt sie en noch ab mit em Greid, un aa noch en Muschter em Granz nooch, as sie sehne kann wo her zu gwilde. Gwilde is eichentlich der Gwilt, der Baett, un die Leining zammenaehe mit feine, katze Schtich.

Der greescht Eifer vun allem is in der Kich. Rischde fer Gwilding is schier so wichdich wie rischde fer Hochzich. Gwildings sin gute Bletz fer neie Reseede ausbrowiere; un kens will sich biede losse. Yedes will es anner iwwerdreffe mit ihrem

pieces, and there are twenty-five blocks."

"Do you sew all those patches together by hand?"

"Oh, no!" Grace laughs. "I wouldn't have enough patience for that. The quilting is done by hand, but I do all the piecing on the sewing machine. "

"How do you cut all those little patches? Do you fold the cloth together and cut about four at a time?"

"Maybe I would if I were cutting them out of a large piece of cloth. We don't buy new material for most of our quilts, except for the border and lining. I cut most of the pieces out of leftovers from making dresses and aprons. Some of the light-colored material is left over from my baby dresses.

"See, only three patterns are needed for the Morning Star, the small diamonds, the larger triangles, and the big squares. I lay three cardboard patterns on the cloth and cut around them. I can cut the diamonds out of very small remnants."

"Wouldn't it be easier to buy large pieces of cloth and sew them together for a quilt?"

"And waste all those remnants? Besides," Grace's eyes twinkle, "think of all the fun we'd miss."

"Oh, yes, without quiltings, where would you pick up all the gossip?" Menno teases.

"I'd have to depend on you to pick it up at barn raisings," Grace counters. "I hope to be able to sew the blocks together tomorrow, then on Tuesday I can put the quilt into the frame. We have planned the quilting for Wednesday."

If Menno could observe the activities in the Weber home on Tues-

Mariye Schtaenn Gwilt Muschder
Morning Star quilt pattern

Gwilding-Esse. Ken Wunner das so viel Weibsleit uff en Diet sin!

So gschwind wie em Menno sei Scheier faeddich is, will er Vieh neiduh. Es nemmt net lang fer ausmache das es hendiche waer fer uff sei Bauerei wohne. Es hot ken Ursach ferwas sie net heiere sedde, weil der Menno is zweeunzwansich un die Grace eenezwansich. Er schwetzt es mol iwwer mit der Grace, dann mache sie aus fer bis Schpotyaahr heiere. Sie froge die Eldere uff zwee Seide um Rot, awwer es Iwwerich bleibt noch heemlich.

Ungfaehr en Monat eb sie zaehle heiere, geht der Menno een Owed bei dunkel zum Bischof. Er saagt em Bischof wann sie gern heiere deede, uff en Dunnerschtaag, vier Woche vannenaus, aafangs Oktober. Der Bischof is es zufridde, weil der

day, his quilting education would increase. Grace and her mother pin the lining into the quilting frame, the same size as the quilt. Next, they lay fluffy cotton batting on top of the lining, and place the pieced quilt on top, pinning it all together. Then they mark the quilt with chalk, tracing a pattern as a guide for quilting. The actual quilting consists of sewing the quilt top, batting, and lining together with a fine running stitch.

The biggest activity, however, is in the kitchen. Preparations for quiltings are second only to those for wedding dinners. Quiltings are ideal testing grounds for new recipes, besides presenting a challenge of everyone trying to outdo the others in the meals they serve. No wonder so many women are on diets!

When Menno's barn is finished, he is ready to fill it with cattle. It doesn't take him long to decide it would be handier if he lived on the farm. There is no reason why they should not marry, since Menno is twenty-two and Grace is twenty-one. He talks it over with Grace, and they make plans for a fall wedding. The parents on both sides are consulted, but otherwise the plans are cloaked in secrecy.

About a month before the date when they want to get married, Menno goes to see the bishop one evening after dark. He tells the bishop the date they have chosen, on a Thursday four weeks hence, early in October. Since no other couple has taken that date , the bishop agrees.

It now becomes the bishop's responsibility to see that their approaching marriage is published (announced) on the three Sundays preceding the wedding day. According to custom, Menno and Grace do not attend meeting during this time, from the day of their first publishing to the wedding day.

On the Saturday morning following the first publishing, Menno is on the road early with horse and buggy. He picks up Grace, and they deliver all the wedding invitations personally. By Saturday night, about two-thirds of the invitations have

Daatum waar noch net uffgnumme. Es is yetzt em Bischof sei Schuldichkeit fer sarye das sie ausgrufe waerre uff die drei Sunndaage eb der Hochzichdaag. Wie der Gebrauch is, gehn der Menno un die Grace net in Versammling dieweil sie Hochzeiter sin, vun aa das sie es erscht Mol ausgrufe waerre, bis zum Hochzichdaag.

Samschdaag mariyets noch em erschte Mol Ausrufes, is der Menno frieh uff em Weg mit Gaul un Boggi. Erscht laad er die Grace uff, not gehn sie vun Blatz zu Blatz fer die Hochzichleit eilaade. Bis Samschdaag Oweds sin ungfaehr zwee-drittels vun der Leit gheese. Die Iwweriche waerre Sunndaags eiglaade, all as wie die wo zu weit ab wohne, wo bei Brief eiglaade waerre.

Darich die naegscht Woch, un bis zu der Hochzich, is viel Uffruhr in der Weber Heemet. Es ganz Haus muss gebutzt waerre vun unne bis owwe. Die Grace muss ihre Hochzich-Gleeder faeddich mache. Kuche, Pei, un gedreelde Kuche misse gebacke waerre. Fleesch, Gaardesach, un Obscht-Salaat waet grischt. Der Menno un die Grace kaafe Kaendi, Schocklaad-Bars, un Oranges im Schtor. Sie deele selwet die Kaendi Peck un die Schocklaad-Bars aus zu der Geschde. Die Kinner verkaafe die Oranges un es Papkaarn zu der Mannsleit fer zwee Schilling's Schtick; die Weibsleit griege ihres ver nix.

Die Geschde sin all verdeelt in Gruppe, wie es weisst uff der Eilaading. An em Menno un der Grace ihre Hochzich sin dreissich Paar Gheierde, sex Paar Yunge, mit der Brautpaar, drei Hassler, drei Koch, zwee gleene Buwe, un vier gleene Maed. Die gepaaarde Yunge sin gwehnlich vun achtzeh bis vierezwansich Yaahr alt, die Hassler vun vaetzeh bis achtzeh, die Koch es nehmlich, un die gleene Buwe un Maed vun datt nunner. Weil es Webers im Schteddel wohne, hen sie net so viel Blatz fer Geil, so die Hochzich is net ganz so gross.

Die Geschde kumme frieh am Hochzich-Mariye. Die erschde was kumme sin die Hassler, weil sie solle datt sei fer der annere Leit ihre Geil in der Schtall duh. Zwee vun der yung gheierde Mann sin Vorgenger. Sie misse sarye das die Schtiel am Blatz

been given out. A few live far away and receive their invitations by mail; the rest are invited on Sunday.

During the following week and the beginning of the next, there is a bustle of activity in the Weber home, where the wedding is to take place. The family cleans the house from basement to attic. Grace is finishing her wedding dress. They bake cakes, pies, and cookies; and prepare meat, vegetables, and fruit salad.

Menno and Grace raid the store for candies, chocolate bars, and oranges. They will pass out candy bags and chocolate bars personally. The children sell oranges and bags of popcorn to the guests, usually for a quarter each, and pocket the proceeds.

The wedding guests are divided into groups, as designated on the invitations. Menno and Grace have invited thirty (older) married couples, six young (mostly unmarried) couples, three hostlers (chore boys), three cooks who double as waitresses, and two little boys and four little girls. The unmarried couples are usually eighteen to twenty-four years old, the cooks-waitresses and hostlers fourteen to eighteen, and the little boys and girls from four to twelve. Because the Webers live in the village and have less room for horses, there are fewer guests than average.

The guests arrive early on the morning of the wedding. The first to arrive are the hostlers, who will stable the horses for the other guests. Two of the younger married men serve as ushers. It is up to them to place the chairs and seat the guests for the ceremony. Just before the ceremony begins, they also pass cookies and wine to the guests (one wee glass per guest).

Before the wedding begins, Menno and Grace are upstairs, with the other young couples and the cooks-waitresses. The hostlers would be upstairs, too, but they have to take care of a latecomer's horse.

The bishop and deacon with their wives, flanked by the parents of the bride and groom, sit at the front of the main room. The first two rows of chairs are reserved for the young couples

sin, un fer die Leit setze. Sie deele aa Kuche un Wei aus zu der Geschde (yuscht en glee Glessli-voll fer yedes) eb die Hochzich aafangt.

Der Menno un die Grace, die finf Paar Yunge, un die Koch sin uff em Schpeicher eb die Hochzich aafangt. Die Hassler waerre aa, wann sie net noch Geil hedde fer weck-duh. Der Bischof un Eldeschde mit ihre Weiwer, un die Eldere uff zwee Seide sitze ganz vanne in der Hauptschtubb. Vannich ihne, gehe sie gedreht, sin zwee Roihe Schtiel, ausghalde fer die Yunge. Hinnich ihne sitze die annere Geschde, die naegschde Freind es vedderscht. Die Iwweriche sitze in der Schtubb newedraa. Wann die Iwweriche all sitze, kumme die Yunge vum Schpeicher: erscht die Brautfiehrer, not der Menno un die Grace, graad vannich em Bischof, un dann die Iwweriche datt newe un hinnedraa.

Die hochzich Zeremonie halt ungfaehr en Schtund un en Halb. Der Eldeschde leest unnerschiedliche Schrifde, wehe der Lehr vun Hauptbedecking, Haar schneide, Gleeder uffziehre, un die Schuldichkeide zwische Mann un Weib. Der Bischof gebt en Vordraag uff yedes vun der Schrifde. Dann fiehrt der Bischof die Zeremonie aus, un versiegelt ihre Verschpreche mit die rechtse Hend zamme-fasse, unne Kuss odder Hochzichring.

Middaags sin die sex Paar Yunge am Disch in der Kammer. Der Bischof un sei Fraa, die Eldere, un die naegschde gheierde Freind esse in der Schtubb, un die Kinner in der Kich. Die Iwweriche waarde bis es naegscht Mol rum. Es Esse is abaddich gut. Es is gut fer net zu viel vun ee Satt nemme, weil es hot viel Sadde. Es Esse fangt aa mit en ruhich Gebet, un am End en Lied un en laut Gebet.

Die Geschde schpende der Nochmiddaag mit singe, bsuche un noch meh esse. Papkaarn, Oranges, Kaendi, un Lemonade mache's en frehliche Zeit. Es menscht vun der Gheierde gehn heem schpot im Nochmiddaag, un die Yunge bleiwe fer's Nachtesse, un singe un schpiele nochher. Wann die Geschde heemgehn, gebt's en wennich Zarres, weil die Hassler un die

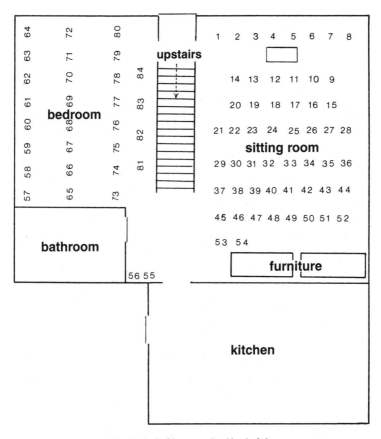

Wo die Leit Sitze an der Hochzieh
Seating plan at the wedding service

1. Em Menno sein Daed/Menno's father
2. Der Grace ihren Daed/Grace's father
3. Der Eldeschde/the deacon
4. Der Bischof/the bishop
5. Em Bischof sei Fraa/the bishop's wife
6. Em Eldeschde sei Fraa/the deacon's wife
7. Der Grace ihre Maem/Grace's mother
8. Em Menno sei Maem/Menno's mother
9-10. Die Brautfiehrer/couple leading the bridal party
11. Der Menno/Menno
12. Die Grace/Grace
13-20. Die iwweriche leddiche Paare/other couples
21-52. Die negschde Freind/the next of kin
53-84. Die iwweriche Geschde/other guests

Geschde Haarschpalde iwwer der Hassler ihren Lohn fer die Geil versarye. Gwehnlich griege sie zwische zwee un drei Daaler.

Der Menno un die Grace gehn net fatt uff en Hochzeitrees, weil sie graad aafange welle haushalde noch der Hochzich. Hoffentlich sin sie uff en lange Hochzeitrees darich ihre ganz Lewe. Des mecht unglaablich laude; doch kumme wennich fehlhafde Ehen zum Vorschein unnich der Mennischde. Loss uns sehne was die Ursach sei kennt, wann des aushalt.

Verleicht hot es en Deel wo net zweegkumme deede, yuscht weil sell net fer gut aagsehne waet, halde sie es bei sich selwer. Sell kennt sei. Wann sell so is, dann halde sie es gut unnich em Deckel—un finne waahrscheinlich Zufriddeheit dabei.

Es waer mieglich das sie besser browiere, weil sie wisse das sie sich net losmache kenne darich Ehescheides. Des waer mieglich. Es is gewiss das die Freind un die Gmee ihne beischteh deede. In en Gsellschaft wo Ehescheides en gwehnliche Sach is, waet oftmols gheiert yuscht fer es ausbrowiere. Wann es net schafft, kenne sie immer noch scheide.

Es mecht sei das sie ken Zeit hen fer bekimmert waerre wehe ihre gheierde Umschtende. Der Mann schafft draus uff der Bauerei. Die Fraa is gscheftich im Haus, die Famillye uffziehe. Langweile is die Ursach fer viel uffgebrochene Ehen. En gschefdicher Bauer, un en Maem mit en grosse Famillye, hen ken Zeit fer Langweil. Verleicht is die Ursach an die anner ghenkt. Wo en grosse Famillye is, bind sie sich zamme darich die Kinner. Sex Kinner sin en gwehnliche Sach bei der Mennischde, un zwelf sin net ungwehnlich.

Yunggheierde Mennischde hewe ihre Pflichde heecher wie die Blessier. Es is verleicht woll mieglich fer falle fer epper Fremms un graad heiere, yuscht es is graad so mieglich fer en friedlich gheiert Lewe fiehre mit em Nochber sei Dochder. Sie mecht verleicht net die schenscht-guckich sei, awwer sie mecht graad so en gude Fraa sei. Es hot ken Schrift fer saage das een besonders Maedel gezaehlt is fer yeden Buh, ausgnumme noch

from upstairs, and Menno and Grace will be in the in the front. Behind them, the other guests are seated in order, with the closest kin nearest. The rest sit in the adjoining bedroom. When all are seated, the couples file down the stairs and take their seats. Menno and Grace sit in the center of the front row, directly in front of the bishop.

The marriage service with the ceremony lasts about an hour and a half. The deacon reads several portions of Scripture that teach on the women's veiling, adornment, hair cutting only for men, and the relationship between husband and wife. The bishop speaks on each subject, then performs the rites with only a joining of hands to seal their vows. There is no kiss or wedding ring.

At dinnertime, the six young couples with Menno and Grace eat at a table in the downstairs bedroom. The bishop, the parents, and the closest kin among the married couples eat in the sitting room, and the children eat in the kitchen. The rest wait for the second round. The feast does credit to its name. It is well to take small helpings, since the variety is great. They begin the meal with a silent grace and end it with a hymn and a prayer.

The guests spend the afternoon singing, visiting, and snacking. Popcorn, oranges, candy, and lemonade help to create a festive air. Late in the afternoon, most of the married couples leave for home; the younger generation stays for the evening feast, with more singing and games afterward. As the guests leave, there is considerable bantering as hostlers and guests haggle over the hostlers' fee. The final agreement is usually between two and three dollars per horse.

Menno and Grace do not leave on a honeymoon, since they start housekeeping within a week after the wedding. We like to assume that they have an extended honeymoon throughout their married life. This may sound unrealistic. Yet few unsuccessful marriages become evident among the Mennonites. Why is this true?

em Heiere, wo dann nimme gewexelt waerre daerf.

Es waer glaablich das die Hauptursach fer en glickliches gheiert Lewe aa liegt in der Goldene Regel ausfiehre. Wann der Mann duht zu seiner Fraa wie er geduh hawwe will, un die Fraa es nehmlich zu ihrem Mann, is en gude Gleyeheit fer en glickliches gheiert Lewe fiehre. Wann es noch sogaar letz geht, un sie kumme nimme zweeg, macht's en Unnerschied wann die Blatt sich dreht.

So war die Sach wehe en vergnuddede Fraa un ihren unbekimmerde Mann. Sie sin yuscht nimme zweegkumme minanner. Dann sin sie zu em Rotgewwer gange. Er hot sie eens bei eens in sei Schtubb gnumme.

Zu der Fraa hot er gsaat, "Wann dir minanner in mei Schtubb kummet, saag was du gehe ihn hoscht, un seh mol was er saagt."

Zu dem Mann hot er gsaat, "Wann dir minanner in mei Schtubb kummet, was-ewwer dei Fraa saagt, saag yuscht, 'Du mechscht recht sei.'"

Wo er dann die Paar minanner neigebrocht hot, un die Fraa hot aagfange gnuddere, hot der Mann gsaat, "Du mechscht recht sei." Noch em dritte Mol rum hot sei Fraa gmehnt, "Saag! Was fehlt dir?"

Sie hot nix meh ghat zu saage. Es waar nix meh zum zaerfe. Eenichkeit un Zaerferei sin wie Wasser un Eel. Sie gehn net minanner. Es hot ihne gwisse des es helft fer em annere sei Gfiehl in Acht nemme.

Darich der erscht Winder uff ihre Bauerei bringe der Menno un die Grace ihre Zeit zu mit zweegmache un iwwerschaffe, nooch un nooch. Die Grace zaehlt mehner Eimaches duh wie die voriche Leit hen, so es braucht Laade im Keller. Sie will aa mehner Blatz fer Gleeder uffhenke, so der Menno baut en Gleeder-Schtiwweli in ee Schlofschtubb, un dreht Hoke in die Wand vun en annere.

Die lange Winder Owede waerre langweilich zu Leit wo gegwehnt sin fer Television gucke alle Owed. Der Menno un die

Some marriages may be in trouble, but since this is not an accepted standard, the sufferers keep it to themselves. If this is true, they must be deceiving the public—and they may still be working at restoring their marital relationships and enjoy life more by doing so. Perhaps they try harder to get along because they believe marriage is to be lifelong. They certainly enjoy the support and encouragement of their relatives and the church community. In a society where divorce is accepted and commonplace, marriage may be approached on a trial basis: if the marriage doesn't stick, divorce is an escape valve.

Mennonite couples may be too busy to worry about marriage problems. The man has his work on the farm. The wife is busy in the house, raising the family. Boredom is one of the causes of broken homes. A busy farmer and the mother of a large family are never bored.

Where there is a large family, there is a common bond in the children. I say "large," since the average Mennonite family has about six children; some families even have a dozen children.

Mennonite couples value commitment more than romance. It is possible for a marriage to result from love at first sight, but it is just as possible to have a satisfactory marriage relationship with the girl next door. She may not have been the campus belle, but she may be just as good a wife and mother. There is no scriptural support for the idea of a "one and only" partner except after marriage, when the decision has been made.

The main reason for happy marriages may lie in observing the golden rule. If the husband does to his wife as he wishes to be done by, and the wife does likewise to her husband, the chances are favorable for a happy married life. Even in adverse cases, when marriage has practically hit the rocks, a reversal of attitudes can work wonders.

Take the case of the nagging wife and her callous husband. They just couldn't seem to get along, so they went to see a marriage counselor. He called them into his office separately.

Grace denke gaar net an sell. Sie gewwe nix drum wann sie aa in es Bett gehn an der nein Uhr odder frieher. Gwehnlich lese sie noch en Schtund eb sie in es Bett gehn. Wiewol das die Biewel erscht kummt, hen sie noch genunk anner Leses. In ihre Zeidingreff is die *Family Life*, die *Young Companion*, *Die Botschaft*, so das sie lese kenne vun Freind in der Schteets, un die lokal Zeiding.

Mariyets un Oweds helft die Grace em Menno mit der Schtallaerwet. Deel Meed wo im Schteddel uffwaxe, wedde net in der Scheier schaffe. Die Grace is froh mit was sie laent dabei. Dodernewe gebt es noch mehner Zeit fer beinanner sei.

Die yung Paar find glei aus das es deier is fer es Fleesch alles kaafe fer uff der Disch. Der Menno kaaft dann en yunge Loos an der Stockyards, un en Vaeddel Kuhfleesch vun seim Daed. Sie sin net eigricht fer daheem butschere, so sie mache aus mit seinere Eldere fer bei ihne butschere.

Em Menno sein Daed hot en Kuh gschlacht Muundaag mariyets, weil sie aa Fleesch gebraucht hen. Nochmiddaags gehn es Mennos niwwer fer ihre Vaeddel uffschaffe. Erscht lese sie en Paar scheene Rooscht raus, dann metzle sie es iwwerich Kuhfleesch ab vun der Gnoche. Wann die Gnoche all haus sin, schneide sie es Fleesch in Rieme, un maahle es mit der Waeschtmiehl.

Der naegscht Mariye schtehn sie frieh uff, so das sie ihre

To the wife, he said, "When you come into my office together, tell me your grievances, and we will see how he reacts."

To the husband, he said, "When you come into my office together, whatever your wife says, answer, 'You may be right.' "

When he brought the couple in together, the wife started complaining; the husband replied, "You may be right." After the third round of this, the wife exclaimed, "Say, what's wrong with you anyway?"

She was deflated. There was no more point in arguing. Agreement and argument are like oil and water: they don't mix. They were learning that self-discipline in considering the needs and feelings of the spouse would help to reshape their attitudes.

During the first winter on their farm, Menno and Grace spend most of their spare time repairing and renovating the house by degrees. There are shelves to put up in the cellar; Grace intends to do more canning than the former owners had done. Grace would also like to have more room for hanging clothes, so Menno builds a clothes closet in one bedroom and puts coat hooks on the wall of another.

The long winter evenings would be boring to those who are used to watching television for several hours every night. Menno and Grace have no such thoughts. They have no objection to going to bed at nine o'clock or earlier.

Usually they read for an hour before going to bed. Although the Bible comes first, they have other types of reading material. Their paper rack holds *Family Life, Young Companion,* and the local newspaper. The *Botschaft* keeps them informed about the activities of friends across the border.

Morning and evening, Grace helps Menno with the chores. Some women would object to working in the barn if they were not raised on the farm, but Grace values the education she receives by helping. Besides, it allows them more time to spend together.

The young couple soon discovers that it is expensive to buy

 Mariye-aerwet faeddich hawwe kenne un niwwer faahre bis acht Uhr. Wann sie annekumme, is es Wasser im Kesseloffe schunn am koche. Der Menno geht in der Schtall un macht en Schtrick fescht an der Loos ihrem Beh, un fiehrt, odder yaagt sie naus in der Scheierhof. Er rollt sie uff ihren Buckel, un hebt sie drunne. Der Daed schtecht sie in der Hals mit en lang, scharf Messer. Wann sie dod geblude hot, rolle sie die Loos in der Briehdrog, un reiwe ihre Haut mit Rassem. Sell gehl Schtofft bappt die Haer zamme, das sie all abkumme in Schiwwel. Yetzt scheppe sie kochich Wasser aus em Kessel in en Weschzuwwer un draage es naus fer iwwer die Loos leere. Mit Kedde rolle sie die Loos riwwer un niwwer so das die Haut net verbrieht. Bis dann kumme die Baeschde leicht ab. Wann es menscht vun der Haar ab sin, henke sie die Loos uff die Seigalye un schiewe sie nuff fer sie ausnemme.

Der Menno saegt der Kopp un die Fiess ab, un nemmt sie nei in es Weschhaus fer sie schaawe. Wann die Baeschde all ab sin, schmeisst er es Fleesch in der Kessel. Unner daereweil nemmt der Daed die Loos aus un saegt sie langs darich der Rickschtrang. Not draagt er sie nei in es Weschhaus, un schnitzelt die Schunke un Rooscht raus. Die Schunke waerre in Salzwasser uffgweecht un not gschmokt, un die Rooscht waerre eigwickelt fer gfriere.

Bis des Zeit hot's aa Aerwet fer die Grace un em Menno sei Maem. Sie schwaarde es Fleesch ab, un schmeisse die Schwaarde in der Kessel mit der Lewwer un es Koppfleesch, fer Lewwerwaescht mache. Sie schneide der Schpeck in Gletzlin, wo not ausgebrode waet fer Fett. Ennich Fleesch was schunscht net gebraucht is waet abgmacht vun der Gnoche un in Rieme gschnidde fer maahle—en Deel fer zum gmaahlene Kuhfleesch fer Biefwaescht, un es Iwwerich fer Brotwaescht.

Yetzt muss gnau geplaennt waerre fer es bescht Yuus mache vun em Kesseloffe un der Waeschtmiehl. Verleicht hot es noch

all the meat for the table. To offset this, Menno buys a young sow at the stockyards and also arranges to get a quarter of beef from his father. He does not have the facilities for butchering, so they plan to butcher at the home of Menno's parents.

After Menno's father slaughters the cow on a Monday morning, in the afternoon Menno and Grace go over to cut up their quarter. They take their sow along and pen her in the stable. First, they pick out a few choice roasts; then they trim meat from the bones of the rest. When they have removed all the bones, they cut the meat into strips and run it through the meat grinder.

The next morning they rise extra early so they can do their chores and drive over to be there by eight o'clock. When they arrive, the water is boiling on the kettle stove in the summer kitchen. This is a huge cast-iron kettle placed on a cut steel barrel, with openings so a fire can be built below to heat the water.

Menno goes to the stable to rope the sow and bring it out into the yard. He holds the sow down while his father puts it to sleep and bleeds it. Then they roll it into the scalding trough and rub the skin with resin, which sticks the hairs together and will make them easier to remove.

Next, they dip the boiling water out of the kettle into a washtub and carry it out to pour over the pig. With the aid of chains, they roll the sow back and forth to prevent scalding the skin. By this time, the bristles come off easily. When most of the hairs have been removed, they push the pig up on the pig hangers or gallows, to remove the insides.

Menno cuts off the head and feet and takes them to the washhouse for scrubbing. When all the bristles have been removed, he throws the meat into the hot kettle. Meanwhile, his father cuts the carcass down the center and carves out the hams and roasts. Later they soak the hams in brine and hang them in the smokehouse. They wrap the roasts for freezing or can them.

Zeit fer es Biefwaescht Fleesch schaffe. So gschwind wie es Lewwerwaescht Fleesch weech is, waet's aus em Kessel gnumme un nausgschtellt fer abkiehle, un es Fett in der Kessel gleert fer ausbrode. Der Menno maahlt es Biefwaescht Fleesch es zwett Mol, un der Daed rischt es Gwaetz. Die Grace riehrt es Fett dann un wann so das es net aabrennt.

Wann es Biefwaescht Fleesch gmaahle is, maahlt der Menno es Brotwaescht Fleesch, dieweil der Daed es Gwaetz in es Biefwaescht Fleesch schafft. Die Grace un ihre Schwiegermaem lese die Gnoche aus em Lewwerwaescht Fleesch, wo not reddi is fer maahle so gschwind wie die Brotwaescht faeddich sin.

"Hot's noch Zeit fer die Biefwaescht schtoppe eb es Fett reddi is?" frogt der Menno.

Der Daed drickt en Brocke Fett mit der Gawwel. "Ich glaab net; awwer verleicht kennte mir die Brotwaescht noch schtoppe. Sell nemmt net lang."

Der Menno fillt der Schtopper, un der Daed schtrefft die Daerm an der Schpaut. Der Menno dreht der Haendel, un die Waescht gringele sich uff der Disch darich em Daed sei erfaahrene Hand. Wann die Waescht gschtoppt sin, rischt der Menno der Schtopper fer Fett auspresse, un der Daed holt der anner Kessel raus fer es hees Fett neipresse. Der Menno dreht, un der Daed scheppt es hees Fett in die Maschien. Es schtiemt net, awwer der Menno weest as Fett viel heeser is wie kochich Wasser.

So gschwind wie es Fett aus em Kesseloffe kummt, geht es Lewwerwaescht Fleesch nei, mit genunk Fleeschbrieh fer leicht riehre. Die Grace riehrt es Fleesch bschdendich so das es net aabrennt. Der Menno un sein Daed schtoppe die Biefwaescht in Seck. Es is hadde Aerwet, weil die Waescht misse hatt gschtoppt sei so das sie sich halde. Der Daed duht es Gwaetz an die Lewwerwaescht un versucht sie als widder bis sie recht schmacke.

Es waet dunkel. Die Grace schtaert uffwesche—der Schtopper, die Miehl, Ziwwer, un Messere. Die Mannsleit scheppe es

By this time, there is work for Grace and Menno's mother. They skin off the rinds and toss them into the kettle with the liver and head meat, for headcheese or liver sausage. They remove the fat and cut it into cubes for rendering into lard. Any meat that has not been selected for other purposes is removed from the bones and cut into strips for grinding. Some will go with the ground beef for summer sausage, and the rest is for pork sausage.

At this stage, it takes planning to make the best use of the kettle stove and the meat grinder. There may be time to mix the summer sausage now. As soon as the headcheese meat is tender, they remove it from the kettle and set it out to cool. They dump the fat into the kettle for rendering. Menno runs the summer sausage meat through the grinder the second time, while his father prepares the seasoning. Grace stirs the lard occasionally to prevent burning.

After the summer sausage meat is ground again, Menno grinds the pork sausage while his father mixes the seasoning into the summer sausage. Grace and her mother-in-law remove the bones from the headcheese meat, which is ready for grinding as soon as Menno finishes with the pork sausage.

"Is there time to stuff the summer sausage before the lard is ready?" Menno asks.

His father tries a piece of fat with a fork.

"I hardly think so. Perhaps we can stuff the pork sausage, though."

Menno fills the stuffer while his father strips the casings on the spout. Menno turns the crank, and the sausages curl in a neat circle on the table, guided by Father's experienced hand. When all the sausages have been stuffed, Menno prepares the stuffer for pressing lard. His father gets out the other kettle for the rendered lard. Menno turns the crank, while his father dips the hot lard into the machine. There is no steam, but Menno knows that the lard is hotter than boiling water.

As soon the lard is all out of the kettle, the headcheese meat

Fett un die Lewwerwaescht in Heffe, Kiwwel un Kanne. Wann der Bodde gwesche un gfeegt is, laad der Menno es Fleesch uff, un sie gehn heem mit ihre Lood. Die Grace hot noch viel Aerwet der naegscht Daag, wo der Menno helft was er kann. Die Brotwaescht un en Deel vum Fleesch misse in Tschaers geduh waerre fer schtieme. Es iwwerich Fleesch waet eigwickelt fer gfriehre. Die Grace hot noch net viel Erfaahring mit dem, awwer sie frogt ihre Schwiegermaem so viel wie sie kann. Sie hofft yuscht das ihre erscht Mol Browieres fer Fleesch versarye schafft gut aus.

Der Gaarde un Bammgaarde hen ihren bedeidender Blatz in der Mennischde Bauere ihre Heemede. Es waare en Paar alde Eppelbeem im Bamgaarde wo der Menno sein Blatz grickt hot. En halb Dutzet Rhubarb Schteck, zwee Sauerkaesche-Baem, un en Bierebaam waare der Fens nooch. Der Menno hot browiert die Baem butze, weil die Grace guckt vaerre fer ihre eeye Obscht hawwe. So gschwind wie es Frieyaahr kummt, helft der Menno der Grace en Roi Aebeere un en Roi Hembeere aablanze.

Wann die Grace der Gaarde blanzt, denkt sie net yuscht an frisch Gaardesach fer uff der Disch. Sie denkt aa vun Gaardesach un Obscht fer naegscht Winder. So gschwind wie der Gaarde drucke genunk is, blanzt sie Selaat, Aerbse, un Reddich fer Friegaardesach. En Woch odder so schpeeder blanzt sie es Haupt fer eimache.

Des Eimaches fangt aa wann es erscht Sach zeidicht: aa vorher, weil der Rhubarb is reddi bis der erscht Yuni. Die Grace macht en Deel ei alleenich fer Pei, un es Iwwerich mit Peineppel, fer en bessere Gschmack mache. Die Zeit fer eimache halt aa darich der ganz Summer, wann die Aerbse, Bohne, Welschkann, un Tomeetoes zeidiche.

Weil noch net genunk Obscht im Gaarde un Bammgaarde is, kaaft der Menno en Kiwwelvoll schwatze Siesskaesche un

is dumped into enough water and gravy for easy stirring. Grace is enlisted to stir the meat constantly. Meanwhile, Menno and his father stuff the summer sausage into cotton bags. It is hard work: the sausages have to be stuffed tight so that they will keep. Father seasons the headcheese, sampling it occasionally until the right flavor is obtained.

Darkness has fallen. Grace starts washing up the stuffer, grinder, tubs, and knives. The men dip the headcheese and lard into crocks, pails, and cans. After they scrub the floor of the summer kitchen, Menno loads the meat, and they head for home with their precious load.

More work awaits Grace the following day, although Menno helps all he can. The sausages and some of the stewing meat must be put into sealers (glass canning jars) for steaming. The rest of the meat is wrapped for freezing. Grace has not had much experience in all this, but she finds out as much as she can from her mother-in-law. She can only hope that her first attempt at meat preserving may be successful.

Garden and orchard play important roles in the Mennonite farm home. There were a few old apple trees in the orchard when Menno took possession of the farm. Along the fence ranged half a dozen rhubarb plants, two sour cherry trees, and a pear tree. Menno makes an attempt at pruning the trees; Grace looks forward to having fruit of their own. As soon as spring comes, Menno helps Grace plant a row of strawberries and one of raspberries.

When Grace plants her garden, she thinks of fresh vegetables and fruits for the table, and vegetables and fruit to can for next winter's use. As soon as the garden is dry enough, she sows lettuce, peas, and radishes for early harvesting. A week or so later, she plants the main crop for canning.

Canning begins when the first crop ripens. Rhubarb is ready by the first of June. Grace cans some of it plain, for pies, but

zwee Buschel Paesching. Newich dem griege sie noch en halb Buschel Blaume aus em Menno sei Eldere ihrem Bammgaarde. Wann des alles versarigt is, guckt die Grace iwwer ihren Laader im Keller mit Vergniege. Sie brauche net verhungere in ihrem erschde Yaahr uff der Bauerei.

"Glopp, Glopp, Glopp!"

"Es laut wie wann epper an der Daer waer, Menno," bischpert die Grace.

Wie der Menno sich aaziegt, guckt sie an der Wecker. "Halb elf! Eppes muss letz sei!"

Die Grace heert der Mannsleit ihre niddere Schtimme ausser an der Daer, awwer sie kann die Wadde net verschteh.

"Wer is es?" frogt die Grace wann der Menno zrick nei kummt.

"Der Levi." Der Menno schluckt hatt. "Er bringt Watt vum Hoschbidaal. Der David Bauman is umkumme."

"Der David—unser Breddicher?" Der Grace ihre schlofiche Sinne kenne es ball net begreife.

"Er waar am Granke bsuche un hot im Schteddel gschtoppt uff em Heemweg, un es is dunkel waerre. En Bsoffener hot sei Boggi gedroffe vun hinnebei. Sie hen ihn ans Hoschbidaal gnumme, awwer er hot yuscht noch en Schtund glebt."

Der naegscht Mariye schicke es Mennos sich mit der Mariye-Aerwet un gehn an es Schterbhaus. En Deel vun der eldere Leit waare am Leicht plaenne. Eens vun der Mann dreht sich zum Menno.

"Kennte dir helfe am Haus?"

"Oh, ya, mir welle helfe was mir kenne."

"Was ich mehn, epper muss vorgeh. Dir hend ken Kinner, not daed es besser schicke fer eich. Dir waeret gezaehlt fer vorgeh am Schterbhaus, un die Grace soll vorgeh am koche un rischde."

"Mir hen awwer noch so wennich Erfaahring."

she adds pineapple to most of it to add flavor. The canning season lasts through the summer as peas, beans, corn, and tomatoes ripen.

Since there is not enough fruit in garden and orchard yet, Menno buys a twenty-pound pail of cherries and two bushels of peaches. Besides these, Menno's parents donate half a bushel of plums out of their orchard. When all of these are canned, Grace surveys her cellar shelves with satisfaction. They need not go hungry during their first year on the farm.

"Knock! Knock! Knock!"

"Menno, it sounds as if someone is at the door," Grace whispers.

As Menno is dressing, she looks at the alarm clock. "Ten-thirty! Something must be wrong!"

Grace hears the men's low voices as Menno answers the door, but she can't understand the words.

"Who is it?" Grace asks, as Menno returns to the bedroom.

"Levi." Menno swallows the lump in his throat. "He just brought word from the hospital. David Bauman passed away."

"David—the preacher?" Grace's sleepy mind cannot comprehend the meaning of Menno's words.

"He had been visiting the sick and was driving home after dark. A drunk man drove his car into the back of David's buggy. They took his crumpled body to the hospital, but he only lived another hour."

The next morning Menno and Grace hurry with their chores and go over to visit the bereaved family. Several older people are helping with funeral arrangements. One of the men turns to Menno.

"Can you help at the house?"

"Oh, yes, we want to help what we can," Menno replied.

"Someone has to direct the funeral arrangements here at the house. You and Grace have no children, so it would be easier

"Sell is der Weg fer Erfaahring griege. Ennichweg, mir finne epper fer eich helfe."

Die Leicht waet geplaennt fer nein Uhr am Haus, zwee Daag schpeeder. Der Menno guckt davor das yuscht die naegschde Freind un Nochbere an es Haus kumme. Er hot en Lischt vun Neeme fer weise wie sie der Roi nooch sitze solle an der Leicht, un bei der Leichtfuhre. Er un sein Helfer schtelle die Schtiel in der Schtubb. Es errinnert der Menno an sei Hochzich; awwer die Umschtende sin so annerscht!

So wie die Freind un Bekannde kumme, binne die Hassler (Nochber's Buwe un yunge Menner), die Geil an die Riggelfens hinnich der Scheier. Der Menno weist die Freind in die hinnerscht Schtubb fer der David sehne in der Laad. Es hot Weck un Kaffee uff em Disch fer die wo weit beikumme.

Wann der Menno un sein Helfer die Freind an ihre Sitz gwisse hen, un die katz Breddich fangt aa, gehn sie naus un sariye das die Fuhre in der rechde Addning kumme. Der Breddicher geht vor. Dann kummt en Karitsch mit em hinneschde Sitz hunne, un der veddersch Sitz in der Heeh, fer die Laad faahre. Es naegscht kummt die Famillye, die Draeger, un die annere Freind.

En halb Schtund schpeeder, wann die Breddich verbei is, weist der Menno die Draeger darich die Daer, bis die Laad am Blatz is uff der Karitsch. Der Menno faahrt mit em Fuhrmann uff der Karitsch. Die Grace bleibt am Haus fer helfe rischde fer Middaag.

Wann die Leicht an es Versammlinghaus kummt is der Hof schunn voll mit Leit un Fuhre, awwer es is Blatz glosst beim Graabhof-Dor fer die Leicht-Fuhre aabinne. Der Kehrteeker schtellt en Bank naegscht zum Dor wo die Draeger die Laad druffschtelle. Die Famillye schteht uff ee Seit zrick, un losst die Leit hiwwer un driwwer an der Laad verbeilaafe fer ihn sehne. Der Menno glaabt es kennde en dausend Leit an der Laad verbei laafe, weil der Breddicher David Bauman bekannt waar bei viel Leit.

for you than for some. You would be expected to act as usher at the house, and Grace would help to superintend the cooking and preparing."

"I don't feel very experienced," Menno demurs.

"That's the way to get experience. Anyhow, we'll find someone to help you."

The funeral is planned to begin at nine o'clock at the house, two days later. Menno expects that only the closest relatives and neighbors will be at the house. He has a list of names to show in what order they are expected to sit for the funeral and to follow in the funeral procession. He and his helper set chairs in the living room. It reminds Menno of his wedding; yet how different are the circumstances!

As the relatives and friends arrive, the hostlers (neighboring boys and young men) tie the horses to the rail fence behind the barn. Menno directs the friends to the back room to view David's body in the coffin. There are buns and coffee on the table so that those who have come a long way can have a bite to eat.

When Menno and his helper have directed all the guests to their seats, and the short sermon has begun, Menno goes out to make sure that the hostlers bring the teams in their proper order. The preacher who is in charge comes first. After him comes a carriage that bears the coffin; the rear seat has been removed and the front seat raised so that the driver sits above the coffin. Next come the immediate family, the pallbearers, and other close relatives.

Half an hour later, when the sermon is over, Menno directs the pallbearers through the doors until they place the coffin on the carriage. Menno rides with the driver of the carriage. Grace stays at the house to help with preparing the meal. When they arrive at the meetinghouse, the yard is crowded with people and teams, but room has been reserved to tie the horses next to the cemetery.

The caretaker places the stand near the cemetery gate. The

Wann die Iwweriche all an der Laad verbei sin, sammelt die Famillye sich nochemol um die Laad rum fer en letschde Blick. Wann sie sich zrickschtelle, macht der Kehrteeker der Deckel zu, un die Draeger draage die Laad naus zum Graab, mit em Breddicher vanne her, un die Famillye un Freind hinnernooch. Sie losse die Laad nunner in's Graab mit Schtrick, un dien der Deckel uff die Rauhlaad. En paar Mann schaufele Grund in es Graab, wo en Lied gsunge waet dabei; not gehn die Drauerleit zrick in es Versammlinghaus.

Die Famillye un naegschde Freind sitze uff Benk vannich em Breddichschtul, un uff die veddeschde Benk uff drei Seide. Die iwweriche Leit sitze wo es basst bis es Haus voll is.

Die Leichtbreddich is viel wie en annere Versammling, yuscht der Eldeschde leest ken Kabiddel ab. Die zwee Breddicher wo Deel hen, erwaehle yedes en Text vun en Paar Vaersch; un nadierlich sin die Lieder wehe em Dod, odder Leicht-Lieder. Am End vun der letschde Breddich leest der Breddicher der Naame un die Elt ab vun em Verschtorwene, un duht en Dank abschtadde fer die Behilflichkeit vun Freind un Nochbere, un macht die Eilaading fer wer will, zrick an es Schterbhaus kumme fer en Schtick Erfrischung zu geniesse.

Der Menno geht bei Zeit widder mit em Fuhrmann vun der Laad-Karitsch zrick an es Haus, so das er bei der Hand is wann die Drauerleit un Freind zrickkumme. Er muss widder helfe die Geschde setze am Disch, noch seiner Lischt. Der Breddicher sitzt am End vun am Hauptdisch, bei der Famillye. Es geht viel her wie an en Hochzich, yuscht es is en Zeit vun Leed in Blatz vun Freed, un es Esse is eefach in Blatz vun iwwerflissich.

pallbearers place the coffin on the stand and open it. The family stands back as a group while the crowd files past the coffin for the viewing, men on one side, women on the other. Menno estimates that over a thousand people view the body. Preacher David Bauman is widely known.

After all the rest have filed past, the bereaved family gathers around the coffin for a final viewing. When they step back, the caretaker fastens the lid down. The pallbearers carry the coffin out to the grave, led by the preacher. They are followed by the family and close relatives—a group of about fifty.

They use ropes to lower the coffin into the grave, which is lined with a rough wooden box. Then they put the cover on the box. As a few young men of the congregation shovel earth into the grave, the song leaders and ministers sing a hymn. Then they all return to the meetinghouse, where the rest of the people are waiting. The family and close friends sit on benches in front of the pulpit, and on the front benches on three sides.

The funeral service inside is much the same as a Sunday church meeting, except that the deacon does not read a Scripture text. The two preachers who take part each select a text of a few verses. The hymns are related to death and funerals. After the last sermon and the closing prayer, the leading preacher gives the name and age of the deceased brother, expresses thanks on behalf of the bereaved family, and invites all those who wish to do so to return to the house of mourning for refreshment and fellowship.

Menno accompanies the driver of the carriage back to the house, so he is on hand when the mourners and friends return. He is expected to help in directing the guests to the table, according to his list. The presiding preacher sits at the head of the main table with the bereaved family. The proceedings are similar to a wedding in many ways, except that it is an occasion of sorrow instead of joy, and the meal is simple instead of sumptuous.

Noch mehner Pflichte auszurichde

UNNERSCHIEDLICHE Monete gehn rum. Es is Zeit fer Umfrog vor dem Nachtmol. Dann waet aa Umfrog ghalde wehe schtimme fer en Breddicher am David Bauman sein Blatz. Die Umfrog is willich fer es vornemme. Dann waet es darich die Zammekunft gnumme, un datt aa eigschtimmt. Not waet der Daag bschtellt fer schtimme.

Der Menno kann es woll begreife das er die Elt hot wo en Deel schunn gschtimmt sin waerre, awwer er macht sich weis das er is noch zu yung un unerfaahre. Wann die Grace es aa noch uffbringt, finnt er es haedder fer es weckschmeisse. Es ruhgt ihm schwaer uff em Gmiet. Was wehe der Grace un ihre drei-woche-alt Bobbi? Waer er es wert fer so en Amt bediene? Kennt er breddiche? Er finnt ken Ruh bis er sich ganz uffgebt.

Fer etliche Woche, un widder am Daag von schtimmes, waet die Versammling vermaahnt zum Gebet fer Gottes Fiehring. Em End vun der gwehnliche Versammling, geht der Bischof un een Eldischde naus in es Rotkemmerli. Eens bei eens, vannich em schtille Haus, gehn vun der eltschde Mann naus fer ihre Schtimm abgewwe. Noch ihre Iwwerzeiging benaame sie der Mann wo sie fiehle wer gschickt zum Amt. Wann sie ken Iwwerzeiging hen, kenne sie aa nausgeh fer der Sege winsche zu em Vornemmes, unne en Naame abgewwe.

Wann es Schtimmes verbei is, gebt der Bischof die Neeme vun der Kandidaade aus. Der Menno is der yingscht unnich nein Schtimme. Der Bischof frogt die Kandidaade un ihre Weiwer fer zammekumme am Versammlinghaus fer Unnersuching

Added Responsibilities

SEVERAL months pass. It is time for counsel meeting to prepare for the communion service. The ministers ask for counsel on the advisability of nominating candidates for a preacher in place of David Bauman. With the approval of the meeting (*Versammlung*, members of the congregation), the ministers take the matter to the conference, where it is also approved. The day is set for taking nominations, choosing candidates.

Menno is aware that he has reached the age at which some have been ordained, yet he tells himself that he is too young and inexperienced. When Grace mentions the possibility, he finds it harder to shrug off. The thought rests like a yoke upon his shoulders. Would he be worthy of such a charge? Would he be able to speak? What about his responsibilities for Grace and their three-week-old baby? Menno finds no rest until he resigns himself completely to God's will.

For several weeks before and again on the day of nominating candidates, the congregation is admonished to pray for guidance. At the close of the service, the bishop and a deacon retire to the counsel room. One by one, amid a hushed congregation, several of the older men of the congregation follow to volunteer counsel. Following inner convictions, each one names a male member whom he feels has the required qualifications. If his convictions do not lead him toward a certain individual, he may offer his blessing on the process without submitting a name.

When nominations have closed, the bishop announces the names of the candidates. Menno is the youngest of the nine candidates. The bishop asks the candidates and their wives to

der negscht Nochmiddaag.

Die Kandidaade gehn aus em Versammlinghaus wie in en Draam. Ausser am Haus sammle sie sich in ruhige Gsellschaft. En Deel Glieder wo schunn so en Erfaahring ghat hen, kumme fer Mut zuschpreche. Die Draene sin naegscht, abaddich bei der Weiwer. Der Schlof is langsam am kumme in der Kandidaade ihre Heemede selle Nacht.

All die Diener un ihre Weiwer, un die Kandidaade un ihre Weiwer, sin beinanner fer die Unnersuching. Die Versammling is net zeremoniel; die Diener un die Kandidaade sin um enanner rum. Die Versammling is im Iwweriche viel wie en gwehnliche, mit dem Text un die Lieder rausglese wie es schicklich is fer die Umschtende.

Der Bischof unnersucht die Kandidaade wehe ihr Zuschtende; eb sie schicklich waere zum Amt, un eb sie willich waere fer sich uffgewwe zu dem was gebraucht is fer es Amt bediene. Der Menno fiehlt schwer belaade, awwer er fiehlt aa die Verbindlichkeit wo er gschpiert hot iwwer em Daafes.

Der naegscht Daag versammle es Mennos sich, mit der annere Kandidaade, an der gwehnliche Zeit in em volle Versammlinghaus. Die Kandidaade sitze uff en Bank graad vannich em Breddichschtul, der Elt nooch, so das der Menno der letscht is. Er denkt draa das sie sitze wo die Drauerleit hen an der Leicht.

Noch en schicklich Lied un Text, red en Breddicher vun der Schuldichkeit als en Breddicher vum Effengelium. Not nemmt der Bischof iwwer, un vermahnt die Glieder so wohl wie die Kandidaade.

Zwee Eldeschde nemme nein gleichene Lieder-Bicher naus in es Rotkemmerli. In eens vun der Bicher is en Babier-Zettel. Sie wexle die Bicher rum, iwwer un iwwer; dann kumme sie rei mit der Bicher un schtelle sie uff der Breddichschtul vannich die Kandidaade.

Em Menno sein Hals waet eng.

Die ganz Versammling gniet im Gebet, wobei der Bischof

assemble at the meetinghouse the following afternoon for examination.

The candidates leave the meetinghouse in a daze. Outside the house, they gather in quiet communion. Several members who have had similar experience offer encouragement. Tears are close to the surface, especially among the women. Sleep is elusive in the homes of the candidates that night. Grace is glad that at least the baby sleeps well.

All the ministers and their wives and the candidates and their wives are present for the examination. The meeting is informal; the ministers mingle with the candidates. The meeting proceeds in the usual way, with appropriate text and hymns.

The bishop examines the candidates regarding their qualifications and their desire to submit themselves to any changes required to qualify. Menno still feels heavily burdened. At the same time, he also feels that close fellowship so evident at the time of his baptism.

On the following day, in front of a full meetinghouse, Menno, Grace, the rest of the candidates, and their wives gather at the regular time of meeting. The candidates sit on a bench directly in front of the pulpit; their wives sit on the front bench of the older women's section. Menno recalls that they sit where the bereaved family of the late preacher sat only a few months before. They sit in order of age; Menno as the youngest is the last in the row.

After a suitable hymn and text, a preacher delivers a sermon on the duties of a preacher of the gospel. The bishop then takes over, exhorting the lay members as well as the candidates.

Two deacons take nine identical hymnals and retire to the counsel room. Into one of the books, they place a slip of paper. After shuffling the books, they bring them in and set them in a row on the pulpit, in front of the candidates.

Menno feels a tightening in his throat.

The congregation kneels in prayer, while the bishop prays as

114 Noch mehner Pflichte auszurichde

bitt wie im Apostelgeschichte 1:24: "Herr, aller Herzen Kindiger, zeige an, welchen du erwehlet hast unter diesen."
Der Bischof wexelt die Bicher nochemol rum, un mit Uffmunderinge Wadde frogt er die Kandidaade fer yedes en Buch nemme, in enniche Addning. Wann yedes en Buch hot, frogt der Bischof sie fer ihre Bicher zrickgewwe, am Eldschde aafange. Er bleddert darich es Buch, un gebt's widder zrick. Wie yede Buch uffgmacht waet, gloppt em Menno sei Haetz. Wann em Menno sei Buch uffgmacht waet, finnt der Bischof der Zettel un leest es: "Das Los wird geworfen in den Schoss; aber es fallt wie der Herr will" (Spriche 16:33).
Der Bischof frogt der Menno fer vaerrikumme un annegniehe, not legt er sei Hend uff em Menno sein Kopp, dieweil er die Wadde vum Eiweihing ausschprecht:

Der Herr hat dich berufen zu einem Arbeiter an dem Evangelium Jesu Christi; sein heiliges Wort und der Rat Gottes vun unsere Seligkeit zu verkindigen. Ich befehle dir nun, das Evangelium zu predigen, die Unbussfertigen zur Busse zu ermahnen, un die Trostlosen zu tresten. Halte an mit Lesen, mit Ermahnen, mit Lehren. Befleisige dich, dich Gott zu erzeigen als einen rechtschaffener and unstrehflichen Arbeiter, der da recht teile das Wort der Wahrheit. Hab Acht auf dich selbst and auf die Lehre. Beharre in diesen Schticken. Denn wo du solches thust, wirst du dich selbst selig machen, und die dich heren. Ich biete dir nun die Hand, un der Kuss des Friedens, und winsche dir Gottes' Segen and Beistand. Amen.

Die iwweriche Diener griesse der Menno im nehmlicher Weg, mit Hand un Kuss, winsche ihm Gottes Sege, mit noch meh droschtreiche Wadde.
Der Menno hot en wennich Sach zu verennere. Er bschtellt graad bleene Gleeder, un en Keep-Iwwerrock. In der Zwischezeit lehnt er Gleeder vun annere Diener.
Er nemmt sein Traekder an en Schapp, fer die Redder uff Schtaal duh. Wann er geht fer es bezaahle, finnt er aus das

in Acts 1:24, "You, Lord, know the hearts of all men. Show which of these you have chosen."

The bishop mixes the books again. With words of encouragement, he asks the candidates to pick a book, not necessarily in the order as they stand. When each has taken a book, the bishop asks them to return the books, beginning at the oldest. He leafs through the book and returns it to the candidate.

With each book opened, Menno's heart gives a lurch. When at last the bishop opens Menno's book and finds the slip, he reads it, "The lot is cast in the lap, but it falls as the Lord wills" (Proverbs 16:33).

The bishop asks Menno to come forward. He places his hands on Menno's head, pronouncing these words of consecration:

> The Lord has called you as a laborer for the gospel of Jesus Christ, to proclaim his Holy Word and God's counsel for our salvation. I command you now to preach the gospel, to call sinners to repentance, and to comfort those who mourn. Continue in reading, admonishing, and teaching. Apply yourself as an honest and blameless laborer for God, rightly dividing the word of truth. Watch over yourself and your teachings; persevere in these things. For when you do this, you shall save yourself and those who hear you. I offer you my hand and the kiss of peace, and wish you God's blessing and assistance. Amen.

The rest of the ministers greet Menno in the same way, wishing him God's blessing and offering words of encouragement.

Menno has a few changes to make. Since his baptism, he has been wearing a *Fliegelrock* to church. Now he immediately orders a new plain suit, as well as an overcoat with attached cape. Meanwhile, he borrows clothing from another minister.

He takes his tractor to a welding shop, to have the tires changed from rubber to steel. When he goes to pay the bill, he finds that it has already been paid.

epper es schunn bezaahlt hot.

Die Grace hot aa Sach zu verennere. Zum Verschtaune finnt sie es leichter wie der Menno. "Die alt electrisch Waeschmaschien hot doch net gut gschafft," dreescht sie sich selwet. "Yetzt hab ich en annere mit en Inschein." Die gleene Verenneringe zu ihre Gleeder schtehn ihre gut aa. Sie is besser zufridde mit ihre bleene Gleeder wie vorher.

Der Menno kann es selwet net verschteh. Er war bissi vorher un hot schaffe misse fer mache das es Geld rumlangt. Yetzt, mit seim neie Amt, schpent er ardlich mehner Zeit am lese, weil er sich noch mehner iewe sett im Deitsche.

Er bsucht die Granke, un hot noch annere Gschefde aus zu richde; un doch grickt er sei Aerwet geduh, un grickt glebt dabei. Wie der aarme Wittfraa ihren Eelgrug, es scheint net all waerre. Verleicht helfe anner Leit mehner wie er draadenkt.

Verleicht duht Der wo die Macht
hot iwwer der Rege un die Sunn
noch en exdraa Sege
darich scheine losse
uff ihn.

Grace, too, comes in for her share of changes. Strange to say, she finds it easier to adjust than Menno.

"The old electric washer was not working too well anyway," she says. "Now I have a new gas-engine washer."

The minor changes in her clothes seem to become her. Grace is happier now with plainer clothes, as expected of a minister's wife. She gives away some of the fancier baby gifts.

Menno was busy before and had to struggle to make ends meet. Now, with his new responsibility, he spends considerable time reading, to brush up on his German and to study the Bible.

He visits the sick and has other church tasks to do, yet he manages to do his farmwork and to survive. Menno finds it hard to explain. Like the poor widow's oil jug, his supply of time and energy never seems to run quite empty. Perhaps other people are helping more than he realizes. Perhaps the God who has control over rain and sun lets an extra blessing shine through on him.

Die Gsellschaft

DIE MENNISCHDE GSELLSCHAFT is net selbschtendich. Doch, noch der Nadur vun dem Mennischde Weg vun lewe, waerre sie als mehner so das sie sich uffenanner verlosse. Wehe der Konsolidiering vun der Schtaat-Schul-System, hen die Mennischde yetzt ihre eegene Schule, mit ihre eegene Lehrer.

Weil die Mennischde als noch ihren Deitsche Gschmack hen fer Brodwaescht, schlachte un rischde sie es menscht vun ihre eeye Fleesch. Ihre eigeborene Eigenschafde vun Schpaarsamkeit un Fleiss halde sie vun reddi-gmacht Ess-Sach un Gleeder kaafe—wo doch net der recht Schnitt hedde.

Die Mennischde brauche alsnoch viel vun der Handwericke vun lang zrick. Es is alsnoch en Schmidtschapp hie un do zu finne darich die Mennischde Gegend, fer Geil bschlagge. Die menschde sin uff Mennischde Bletz. Unnerschiedliche Karitschmacher sin im Gscheft vun Boggis, Karitsche, un Dachwegglin mache.

In deel Umschtende, hot es Schapps wo en Spezial Schtick mache fer en annere Gscheftsmann. Eener biegt Holz fer Boggi Schaefts un Felge mache. En annere hot en Giesserei fer Schnalle mache fer die Saddler, wo aa gschaefdich sin in der Gegend.

Unnich der Mennischde sin aa Leit wo gschickt sin an Schweesses un Maschien-aerwet. Waterloo County Wegge sin bekannt darich ganz Ontario. Annere Bauere-Maschiene, un Schtalling sin graad so gut bekannt. Der altmodisch Kicheoffe, wo schunn lang veralt war, waert widder gmacht in en Mennischde Schapp. Unnerschiedliche Holz Schapps mache Hausrotsach uff die alt Aart, wo yetzt uffgsucht waerre bei der An-

The Community

THE MENNONITE COMMUNITY is not independent. However, because of the nature of the Mennonite way of life, the community is becoming increasingly interdependent, helping each other. Because of school consolidation and worldly trends in the public system, the Mennonites are now operating their own schools, taught by their own teachers.

Since Mennonites have retained their German taste for sausages, they butcher and process their own meats. Their native traits of economy and industry prevent them from buying ready-made food and clothing. The clothing wouldn't be in the right style, anyhow.

The Mennonites still need and practice many of the specialized trades of bygone times. One still finds blacksmith shops scattered through the Mennonite area, for shoeing horses. Most of them are operated by Mennonites. Several carriage makers ply their trade, manufacturing buggies, carriages, and covered buggies.

In some cases, several shops specialize in a certain segment of the trade. One has a wood-bending operation for making buggy shafts and other curved parts. Another has a foundry for casting brass buckles for the saddlery trade, which is well represented in the area.

Among the Mennonites are a number of craftsmen skilled in welding and machine work. Waterloo County farm wagons are known throughout Ontario. Other farm machinery and steel stabling are equally well known. The old-fashioned cast-iron kitchen range had been obsolete for some time; now it is being manufactured in a Mennonite workshop. Several woodwork-

tique Keefer. Es sin aa viel Schreiner gebraucht, weil viel Scheiere gebaut un iwwergschafft waerre.

Die Alt Mennischde Gmee is weit vun vollkumme. Es hot Schwachheide wo die ganze Zeit noochgeguckt waerre misse; ebmols so das es scheint wie wann ken Darichsicht waer. Es mecht gfrogt waerre, "Worum, mit so viel Addninge un Regele, hot es doch noch so viel Schlechtichkeide in der Gmee?"

Sell is en gude Frog. Schmoke un Drinke sin woll ganz verbodde. Wann es aaghalde waet, is es Nachtmol verbodde. Es hot noch Danzes, yuscht es is aa verbodde unnich der Gmeesglieder. Es mechde noch mehner ungschickde Sache gedriwwe waerre wo mer net ausfinnt. Die Glieder scheine net

ing shops provide furniture similar to the colonial style presently in demand by antique dealers. Various carpenters are in keen demand, since so many barns are being built or remodeled. The Old Order Mennonite Church is far from being perfect. There are weaknesses that need constant attention; at times, some seem to have no solution. One may ask, "Why, with so many guidelines and restrictions, are there still evil conditions in the church?" This is a good question.

Smoking and drinking are well under control. The nonmember youth may do some dancing, even on Sunday evenings. There may be more immorality than shows on the surface. Not all church members are true, born-again Christians.

There may be several reasons for this struggle. The so-called guidelines don't solve every problem. For certain sins or misdeeds, excommunication is the answer; yet there are also cases where this may not work. No one is excommunicated merely on suspicion. Before disciplinary action, there needs to be either a confession or definite proof of serious misconduct.

That is why the church might not take counsel and action on certain cases of questionable dealings or lack of brotherly love. When such a person is guilty without confessing and it cannot be proved, the church is considered to have done its duty. The guilt lies between the transgressor and God.

Another reason for difficulty lies in the democratic nature of the church administration, under God; the church does some balancing like that found in any democratic government. Mennonites believe that God is ruling the church through all the members. Yet church order is administered by both the conservative and the more progressive elements. What seems far out to one is quite normal and acceptable to the other. If the church acts arbitrarily, there is danger of rooting out the wheat with the tares. This caution results in an averaging process.

Countless people have viewed the Old Order Mennonites from a distance with envy. They see them as a green oasis in the dreary desert of the world. Peace, harmony, and serenity

all gedreie, widdergeborene Grischde zu sei.
Es mechde unnerschiedliche Ursache sei. Eens davun kennt
noch sogaar sei darich die Richtschnur. Es hot woll en deel
Sinde wo gschtroft waerre bei zrickschtelle, awwer sell schafft
net in yedem Fall. Mir daerf niemand zrickschtelle unne sicher sei vun der Sach. Entwedders muss er sei Schuld bekenne,
odder muss es bewisse waerre als die Waahrheit, schunscht
kann niemand zrickgschtellt waerre. Sell is ferwas das Unehrlichkeit, odder Unliewe net oft
gschtroft waerre. Wann der Mensch es net uffeegend das er in
der Schuld is, un es kann ken sichere Beweis uffgebrocht
waerre, is es gezaehlt das die Gmee hot dann ihre Schuldichkeit
geduh. Dann ruhgt die Schuld zwischich em Sinder un Gott.

Noch en Ursach liegt in der Natur vun der Gmee ihre
Regiering; graad wie mit unser weltliche Regiering. Weil es
regiert waet bei der Leit, is es regiert bei der Schlechde so wohl
wie bei der Gude. Was aus der Weis scheint zu eem, is gut un
recht beim annere. Wann Gwalt gebraucht waet, mecht der
Weeze rausgroppt waerre mit der Drefze. Drum gebt es en
middelmaessiches Gericht.

Viel Leit gucke die Mennischde aa mit Verlange. Sie sehne
sie als en frisch Wasser in en drucke Feld. Friede, Liewe, un
Eenichkeit scheine raus wie en heller Schtraal. Wann sie neecher kumme, verschtaune sie sich.

"Ich daed woll gern sei wie dir," saage sie, "awwer ich kennt
net lewe wie dir dient. Ken Kars, ken TV, un nix!"

So Leit verlange die Blessier unne der Koschde. Sie gucke die
Richtschnur aa als en Fens. Sie hen Bang vun eigschpaet
waerre. Sie welle die Gleyeheit fer naussschpringe wann sie es
leedich sin. Sie kenne es net begreife das der Friede der Blatz
nemmt vun der weltliche Lischde.

Mir kennt die Alt-Mennischde Gmee vergleiche zu em
Schofschtall im Zehede Yohannes. Es hot en Wand um der
Schofschtall, net fer die Schof aus der gude Weed halde, awwer
fer die Welf un die Dieb draushalde.

shine out from its center like a beacon. As they draw nearer, they view it with awe.

"I really admire and envy you people," they say, "but I just couldn't live the way you do. No cars, no television, or anything!"

Such people suffer from claustrophobia. They see the guidelines as a fence around the oasis. They fear the close confines of its welcome greenery. Much as they long for the shelter of the cooling trees, they still desire to retain the privilege to dash out into the burning desert at will. They do not realize that

Die Schtall-daer is immer uff, das sie aus- un eigeh kenne wie sie welle fer weede. Die Welf un die Dieb kenne net zu der Daer nei, not browiere sie fer iwwer die Wand graddele. Wie dumm waer es wann die Schof browiere deede fer die Wand nunnerreise! In Schpeit vun ihre Schwachheide, hen die Alt-Mennischde noch eppes wo dawaert is fer uffhalde. Do is noch en Gsellschaft wo ken Ehebruch hot, odder uffgebrochene Heemede. Yunge Verbrecher, Unheil, Schtehles, Grobheide, un Unmaessichkeit weest mer ball nix davun unnich ihne. Ihre Glieder nemme ken Hilf fer ihre Kinner uffziehe, fer die Alde behalde, fer die wo aus Aerwet sin odder enniche annere Sadde Hilf vun der Owwerichkeit.

So en Erbdeel is gewisslich dawert fer bewaahre un unnerschtitze!

inner peace replaces the desire for worldly lusts.

A parallel could be drawn between the Old Order Church and the sheepfold described in John 10. There is a fence around the sheepfold, not to deprive the sheep of better pasture, but to shelter them from marauding wolves.

The door to the fold is always open to the sheep, so that they can enter and leave at will, to seek pasture. The wolves and thieves cannot enter by the door; they try to enter by climbing the fence. How foolish it would be for the sheep to try to tear down the fence!

In spite of their weaknesses, the Old Order Mennonites have something that is worth striving to maintain. Here is a society with no divorce or similar family problems. Juvenile delinquency, lawlessness, crime, and violence are practically unheard of. As far as is known, there is no drug abuse. Its members accept no help in the form of child allowances, pensions, unemployment insurance, or any other social benefits, because none of these are needed. They take care of themselves and of each other.

Surely, such a heritage is worth protecting and promoting.

Typical Mennonite Terms

Abschnitt = cut off. *Im Abschnitt stehen* = forbidden by the church.

Aerwet = work; Lancaster OOMs say *Arewet.*

Ausrufen = publish; proclaim banns; announce a forthcoming marriage.

Bent (in a building) = one cross section of a barn skeleton.

Benk nausschtelle = to set benches out; the caretaker of the meetinghouse sets spare benches in the aisles when needed.

Blackboard Bulletin = monthly school paper (Pathway Publishers, Aylmer, Ontario).

Botschaft, Die = Old Order Mennonite weekly newspaper published at Lancaster, Pennsylvania. The ultimate in news among Old Order Mennonites and Amish.

Budget, The = Amish and Mennonite weekly newspaper published at Sugarcreek, Ohio, with about 250 correspondents, from almost every state and Canada.

Boggi = open one-seat buggy used by young and middle-aged people.

Cape = (1) a garment worn by all mature women, wide over the shoulders, covering the chest in front, and coming to a point in the back where it meets the belt of the apron (illustrated at end of chap. 1). (2) circular flap of cloth fastened to the collar of a minister's overcoat.

Couple = a "boy and girl" (young man and young woman) who are "going steady" (courting). At a wedding, those who sit at the head table with the bridal pair are also known as couples but may not necessarily be courting.

Dachweggli = covered or roofed buggy used by older people; square boxlike construction, not a folding-top buggy. Lancaster: *Karritsch.*

Deifling = applicants for baptism (from High German, *Taüfling;* related to *Taufe* = baptism).

Diener = servants (of the church); all ministers, including the deacons and bishops.

Family Life = monthly family magazine for plain people (Pathway Publishers, Aylmer, Ontario).

Fliegelrock = three-piece tailored suit worn for baptism and thereafter, until a plain suit is worn; the coat has wings or a swallowtail at the back.

Gnecht = the hired man who lives in as a member of the family, and is usually hired by the year.

Good-bye = to give good-bye is literally to shake hands at parting.

Haetz = heart; Lancaster: *Hatz*.

Hochzeiter = bridal pair, from date of announcement to wedding day (but not afterward).

Hochzich = wedding.

Kammer = bedroom; specifically, the main-floor bedroom used by the parents.

Kandidaade = Those nominated to be in the lot for choosing a minister; Lancaster: *die unner Schtimme*.

Kapp = Cap: (1) Woman's veiling, or prayer covering, made of white organdy or nylon, worn regularly by the women after marriage, by all girls over fourteen during church services, and by many girls regularly after baptism. (2) Man's cap: older men wear straight or box caps in the winter; boys wear flat caps. Lancaster: no caps worn on Sunday. (3) Little girls wear soft caps instead of bonnets in winter.

Karitsch = carriage, a vehicle with two or three removable seats; the heavier ones are pulled by two horses.

Latzhosse = broadfall pants, worn by most of the older men and all the ministers; a flap across the front buttons at the top.

Maad = maid or hired girl, who is usually hired by the year and lives in as a member of the family.

Mutze = plain suit, a three-piece tailored suit with standup collar and swallowtail coat, worn by ministers and men middle-aged or older.

Newehucke = bride leaders, the couple who precedes the bridal party at a wedding. Lancaster: *Brautfiehrer*.

Rassem/Rosin = resin.

Sack coat suit = two-piece suit worn by boys before baptism.

Sauwerschtubb = clean room, guestroom upstairs; room where daughters have their own furniture, dishes, and so on. Lancaster: *Neweschtubb*.

Schnitz = peeled, cored, and quartered apples, like orange slices.

Schnitzing = work bee to peel and cut up apples for drying.

Scout = spy on courting couples, a common practice in some Lancaster areas but discouraged here.

Shawl = garment worn by all mature women while driving; winter shawl is of dark gray or black wool, fringed; summer shawl is of black crimp or similar material.

Schpeicher = upstairs, upper rooms.

Schtetser = visitors from the United States.

Schteetser faahre = taking U.S. visitors from place to place, visiting.

Schtetser Versammlung or singing = special gathering during the week, in honor of U.S. visitors.

Schtubb = room, specifically the parlor or sitting room.

Singdisch = singer's table in Pennsylvania, where song leaders sit during church meetings.

Singing = Sunday evening gathering of young people between the ages of fifteen and twenty-five.

Schpannpett = the tieplate in a building; the purlin or main horizontal timber of a bent.

Umfrog-Rot = inquiry or counsel meeting, twice a year, before communion.

Unnere = Ontario Conference Mennonites, in the 1889 schism, those from the *unteren* = lower end of Waterloo County; now in Mennonite Conference of Eastern Canada.

Versammlung/Versammling = meeting, church service; Lancaster: *Gmee*.

Vorreed = brief opening sermon/message; preface in a book.

Waescht = sausage; Lancaster: *Wascht*.

Waegli = child's play wagon.

Wie gehts? = (pronounced *vee GATES?*) "How do you do?" said while shaking hands in greeting. Lancaster: occasionally "Howdy."

Young Companion = young people's monthly magazine, from Pathway Publishers.

Resources for Pennsylvania German

Beam, C. Richard, editor. *Kleines pennsylvaniadeutsches Wörterbuch. Abridged Pennsylvania German Dictionary.* Kaiserslautern, Germany: Heimatstelle Pfalz, 1970.

_____. "Pennsylvania Dutch Language: An Introduction to the Pennsylvania Dutch Dialect." Lancaster, Pa.: Brookshire Pubns., n.d. A cassette tape with a guide.

_____. *Pennsylvania German Word List.* Morgantown, Pa.: Masthof Press, 1997.

_____. *Pennsylvania German Words in Context.* Millersville (Pa.) Univ.: Center for Pennsylvania German Studies, 1997; second edition in preparation.

_____. *Revised Pennsylvania German Dictionary: English to Pennsylvania Dutch.* Lancaster: Brookshire Pubns., 1991.

_____, editor. "Vocabulary and Folklore of the Pennsylvania German Dialect of Waterloo County, Ontario." Millersville, Pa.: C. Richard Beam, 1994.

Frey, J. William. *A Simple Grammar of Pennsylvania Dutch.* 3d edition. Lancaster, Pa.: Brookshire Pubns., 1985.

Hershberger, Henry J. (Hank), translator. *Es Teshtament.* Pennsylvania Deitsch un English. Published and distributed by author: 3864 Twp. Rd. 162, Sugarcreek, OH 44681 (330-852-4663). The New Testament, in Pennsylvania German.

Der Verfasser

ISAAC R. HORST (der Isaak vun Bergwald) war gebore am Schluss vum erschde Weltgrieg, uff der Sandhiwwel, zwansich Meil nadde vun Berlin, odder Kitchener, Ontario. Weil er net gsund genunk war fer schwere Aerwet, hot er sei Zeit viel zugebrocht mit lese, in Schul un daheem.

Noch dem das er die Selina Bauman gheiert hot, un sie hen en Familye aagfange, hot er sei Zeit zugebrocht zwische aarmseelich Baueres un im Daaglohn schaffe. Fer zwee Yaahr (1966-68) hot der Horst Schul ghalde in der neie Mennischde Schul, wo gegrind war in 1966. Er hot sei acht Yaahr Schuling unnerschtizt mit Briefwexel darich des Volkschulwesen, naemlich Hochschul Englisch un en Schreibkurs.

Die Schriftlaenning hot en Schreibart aagezinnt bei dem Horst. In zwansich Yaahr's Zeit hot er dreiunzwansich Bicher gschriwwe un selwert rausgewwe; acht historische un fuffzeh Kochbicher.

Unnich dennen sin *Separate and Peculiar/Bei sich selwer un ungwehnlich* (1979, 2001), *Conestogo Mennonite Cookbook* (1981), *The Man Who Could Do Anything* (1983), *Wildlife Vittles* (1983), *Why, Grossdaudy?* (1985), *Close-ups of the Great Awakening* (1986), *Until Jacob Comes* (1990), *Breakin' the Fast* (1991) , un *Liedersammling Commentary* (1997). Unnerschiedliche Bicher hot er in Verwaahring bei Amos B. Hoover sei Muddy Creek Farm Library, Denver, Pennsylvaani.

Er hot aa regelmaessicher Schticker gschriwwe an Zeidinge. Viel vun sei Schticker aus der *Mennonite Reporter* sin yetzt zu finne in *A Separate People* (Herald Press, 2000). Er duht alsnoch viel Iwwersetzes, Deitsch zu Englisch, sowie alde Lieder,

The Author

ISAAC R. HORST was born at the close of World War I, on the Sand Hills, twenty miles north of Kitchener, Ontario. Physically unsuited for strenuous exercise, he spent his spare time in reading, at school and at home.

After he married Selina Bauman and children arrived, the family teetered between unsuccessful farming and off-the-farm jobs. Horst taught for two years in the Mennonite parochial school system, established in 1966. He bolstered his elementary schooling with correspondence courses in high school English (grades 9 and 11) and creative writing.

Those extra courses ignited a literary spark in Horst. During a twenty-year period, he has self-published twenty-three books; eight were religious and historical, and fifteen were cookbooks.

His work includes titles such as this volume, *Conestogo Mennonite Cook Book* (1981), *The Man Who Could Do Anything* (1983), *Wildlife Vittles* (1983), *Why, Grossdaudy?* (1985), *Closeups of the Great Awakening* (1986), *Until Jacob Comes* (1990), *Breakin' the Fast* (1991), and *Liedersammlung Commentary* (1997). He also has preserved many of his unpublished books in Amos Hoover's Muddy Creek Farm Library, Denver, Pennsylvania.

Horst wrote regular columns in newspapers and periodicals. Many of his *Mennonite Reporter* columns appear in *A Separate People* (Herald Press, 2000). For over five years, he has helped C. Richard Beam with his *Pennsylvania German Dictionary.* Now in his early eighties, he still enjoys translating texts from German to English: old hymns, manuscripts, and letters, such as the 1,600 letters of Jacob Mensch, with the help of his

Schrifde, un Brief.

Aafangs 1960, hot der Horst es unnersucht fer en neie Alt-Mennisclide Gmee eisetze in der Mount Forest Umgegend, dreissich Meil nadde vun Elmira, Ontario. Sei Famillye waar vun der Erschde wo datt anne gezoge sin 1968. Aafangs 1990, ware vun seiner Familye vun der Erschde Alt-Mennischde wo noch der Chesley Gegend gezoge sin, vaetzich Meil Naddwescht vun Mount Forest. Die zwee Gegende nemme gut zu. Die Mount Forest Gegend hot vier Versammlingheiser, un an Chesley is eens gebaut waerre in 1998.

Nix vun dem hot der Verfasser reich odder beriemt gmacht, yuscht er saagt des Wegbaahne macht ihn meh uffrierisch wie bauere. Nochdem der Horst sich zur Ruh gsetzt hot vun Bauere, hot er sich en Gscheft gmacht vun alde Gebeier abreisse fer Bauholz, fer zehe Yaahr. Gwehnlich hot er en Scheier nunnerglegt mit der Hilf vun en Paar annere alde Bauere.

Der Isaac Horst un sei Fraa, Selina Bauman Horst, hen elf Kinner bei Lewe, vierunsechzich Kindskinner, un zwansich Urenkel. Sie sin Glieder vun der Cedarview Alt-Mennischde Gmee, wo er zur Zeit Kehrteeker war, un dann noch Vorsinger.

Es mecht zum sehne sei ob em Horst sei Buch, *Up the Conestoga*, zu finne waer in en Bicherei. In dem Buch sin richtiche Blicke in die Gschichde vun der Alt-Mennischde ihre Gmeeschaft. Unnerschiedliche Kabbidel helfe fer die Freindschaft vun der alde Ansiedler noochsuche.

grandson. His wife, Selina, is busy making quilts and doing the housework.

In the mid 1960s, Horst explored having an Old Order Mennonite settlement in the Mount Forest area, about thirty miles north of Elmira, Ontario. His family was among the first to settle there in the late 1960s. In the early 1990s, members of his family were with the first Old Order Mennonites settling in the Chesley area, forty miles northwest of Mount Forest. Both new communities are flourishing. Mount Forest has four meetinghouses, and Chesley built one in 1998.

None of this has made the author rich or famous, but he says the pioneering is more exciting than farming. For ten years after Horst retired from farming, he ran a business of dismantling old buildings for salvage. Usually he wrecked a barn with the help of one or two other retired farmers.

Isaac and Selina Horst have eleven children, sixty-four grandchildren, and twenty great-grandchildren. They are members of the Cedarview Old Order Mennonite Church, where Isaac has served as janitor and as a song leader.

You may wish to check a library for Horst's book *Up the Conestoga.* In it, he gives authentic glimpses into the history of the Old Order Mennonites and the surrounding Ontario community. Several chapters help Mennonites trace their roots back to the original settlers.